*How to Get a Dollar's Value
for a Dollar Spent*

Also by Arthur Milton

LIFE INSURANCE STOCKS: THE MODERN GOLD RUSH

How to Get a Dollar's Value for a Dollar Spent

by ARTHUR MILTON

Preface by Ellis Arnall

BELL PUBLISHING COMPANY · NEW YORK

To My Children,
who I trust always will remember
that, while accomplishment for one's
self can be likened to a hallowed vic-
tory, what you can do for others can
be more rewarding. In this country of
ours, opportunity can best be seized
by those who think of others first and
of themselves second.

Preface

Economic freedom is a corollary to personal freedom. From my work as Attorney General and Governor of Georgia, and as Director of the United States Office of Price Stabilization during the Korean Conflict, I know the mistakes, the tensions and the damage to human dignity which come from financial worries. I know, too, that today millions of American families in every income bracket are living from payday to payday. But this does not have to be so. It is possible, given the correct information, for everyone to learn how to buy more of the things he or she really wants—how to get out of debt and stay out—how to provide for college expenses—a new wardrobe, a trip to Europe—how to own one's home, a new car, and even to start a business—all without earning a penny more!

In *How to Get a Dollar's Value for a Dollar Spent*, Arthur Milton furnishes this all-important and vital information. He brings his years of business experience to a clear analysis of a basic problem confronting millions of Americans. He discusses installment buying, loans, mortgages, food buying, stocks and bonds, insurance, and other important subjects, and offers invaluable advice on how to get the best value for one's expenditure. Concrete, easy-to-follow suggestions on the buying of these and other commodities eliminate guess work from your daily economic life and tell you how to get more *living value* from your present income. If you put this information to use, you will have the chance to sit back and relax without the

7

haunting worry of unpaid bills. Whatever your income, whatever your obligations, you will find this book an invaluable guide to freedom from money worries, a guide to spending money wisely.

I heartily commend it to all Americans who wish to achieve economic freedom and who want to get a dollar's value for a dollar spent.

ELLIS ARNALL

Foreword

It is within your power to gather in more money, even if the boss doesn't come through with that ten-dollar raise you—and most of us—think about so much. If you are a businessman, your concern about increased earnings may always be present.

It's up to you to improve your own lot—and you *can* do it. The first step is to know what's going on around you. This book is intended to provide you with the basic information you will require for improving your financial situation and for providing additional comfort and security for your family.

It's your money; so how you spend it, and whether or not you wish to increase your income, is your decision. The chapters following can do no more than explain how your labor is but part of your possible income source, how money saved—and then put to work—produces additional income *for you.*

It's not easy to spend money wisely—but it's not hard. The difference is in each person's attitude, and, most important, in how well informed he may be. Real estate, stocks and bonds, investment groups, bank mortgages and G.I. mortgages, the wide array of life insurance, and so forth—all these investments can work for you to provide additional income or to help you keep what you have. As can the many other forms of insurance and investment that *are* part of your day-to-day struggle with the dollar.

And, you can lose on each of these investments—you may be spending unwisely right now. It's up to you. The first step is for you to find out what is going on. Skilled professional advice in each field is certainly the best way to survive—and get ahead—in the complicated financial situation every one of us lives with today. Here, simply stated and conveniently arranged for your use, is an experienced advisor's report on today's money market.

The phrase "money market" may be strange to many, but it shouldn't be hard to understand. Money is a commodity—as is wheat, or real estate. If you have a charge account anywhere, you are paying for the use of money. If you own a government savings bond—the government is paying you for the use of your money.

The trick is to make *whatever money you have* do the most work for you. That's why this book ranges from charge accounts to loans to real estate to insurance to sensible saving and crazy hoarding to financing your child's college education, to good—and foolish—insurance, and more. This book is, if you wish, your direct, logical, and detailed introduction to your second source of income— where it's your money that works, not you yourself. And, the book is written to be an at-your-finger-tips reference when a "good thing" is offered to you.

First *know!* Then *do!* Fear of making a mistake keeps many of us from earning some economic freedom and security. If you *don't* know what you are doing with your hard-earned money—you have good reason to be afraid.

On the other hand, with patience, common sense and a willingness to make the effort to learn about the money market *which you are in now, whether or not you realize it,* can increase your income by earning more for you— and by reducing your over-payments for the money *you* use.

Contents

1. A Penny Saved

"A penny saved is a penny earned."

During the past hundred and seventy years, millions of American schoolchildren have memorized this little maxim from *Poor Richard's Almanac.*

But if Benjamin Franklin were with us today, he would have to re-write it. The great apostle of thrift couldn't be so conservative. He would have to say—"A penny saved is worth two earned."

Colonial America was growing tremendously in Franklin's time, but the growth hardly was measured in money. It was, rather, a village economy based largely on barter. Money, what there was of it, was deceptively stable. Most American goods were not turned into money until they had crossed the ocean, and virtually the whole proceeds were gobbled up by the nobility and merchant class of England.

So Franklin did not realize how fast money saved, *and invested* in the economy of the growing colonies, would inevitably grow. Franklin valued thrift for its own sake; he was more concerned with the moral effects of prudence and sober moderation on the human spirit than with the desire to accumulate wealth.

Also, Franklin lived a century before income tax. He could not forsee that the day would come when the federal government and many states would take, in income taxes, from 16 to perhaps 77 cents of every dollar in 1964, or 14 to 70 cents of every dollar in 1965 and thereafter of earned income, *while income produced by invested*

13

money could be managed in such a way that it could be *taxed much more leniently* as a capital gain.

Nor could Franklin have envisioned our present life, in which fifteen to twenty million people own common stocks, and many more millions own government bonds and industrial and commercial bonds and debentures, and our myriad ways of saving money and letting it grow. There wasn't any life insurance in this country in Franklin's day. Credit existed; indeed, it was widespread. But it was based solely on the huge shortage of cash; even the rich were not often able to pay cash for everything they needed. They had to engage in barter or make credit arrangements.

No such flowering of credit as we have today would have been possible in Franklin's time. Doubtless he would have considered it the wildest extravagance. Yet, when we get right down to it, the fundamental economic problem of the ordinary man is the same today as it was in Franklin's time.

It's hard to spend money!

At least it's hard to spend it wisely—or even not to spend it stupidly. And since all of us have to spend money everyday, many of us agonize over whether or not we are spending it foolishly.

My own business career and my experience as a lad born to a far from well-to-do family have convinced me that it is much harder to spend money wisely than to earn it. Yet, the rewards of spending money carefully are the greater. For I consider making money by investment a matter of first spending money. Having put in many years working hard on jobs and in businesses where I had to pound the street, I put a sharp distinction between the dollar earned by ordinary toil, physical or mental, and the dollar made by wise investment spending.

By dint of much organization, agitation and painful bargaining, your union gets you an increase package of

$14 a week spread over two years. Perhaps $6 of this is in fringe benefits which, in the long run, may turn out to be more valuable than the $8 in additional wages, because the fringe benefits are not taxed and you must pay at least 16 per cent and perhaps 30 per cent of the $8 in federal income tax. That brings it down to $6.40 or $5.60—spread over two years.

Well, in this book I intend to show you that it is, in general, much easier to add that much to your income or capital by spending wisely than it is to get it from the boss either on your own or through the union.

Of course that's no argument for not getting more money from the boss or not increasing the income from your business if you're self-employed, but it does point up the fact that far too many of us have one-track minds that keep us from seeing golden opportunities. The truth is that it is not only easier to save $5 or $6 a week from a reasonably good paycheck by wise spending than to get that much in a raise, but there also is a fair chance of making the savings grow very fast. For the person with exceptional perseverance and perception, a steady saving of $5 to $10 a week can be made to grow astonishingly.

Now, lest I be accused of being preachy and uncharitable, let me insist right now that I am not talking of those who are trying to support five kids on $75 or $80 a week in today's economy. That's grinding poverty and such persons have little chance of saving a single penny —or of not going heavily into debt. I am talking of the many who go into debt unnecessarily on family incomes of $150 a week and up.

One of the surest indications that most of us are haphazard and wasteful in our spending is that many advertising men agree that almost 70 per cent of all retail sales are what they call *"impulse sales."* That is, the customer hasn't thought of buying until she sees the merchandise in the store. Obeying this belief, advertisers spend millions

on what is called point-of-purchase advertising: illumi-
nated plastic signs, indoor posters, banners, very elaborate
packages and labels, etc. They are convinced that much
of the millions they spend on advertising in newspapers,
magazines, radio and television will be wasted if it is not
followed through to the point-of-purchase. The DuPont
Company not long ago made a rather elaborate study of
this question and came up with the conclusion that in the
past five or six years the proportion of these impulse
sales, out of total retail sales, had gone up very sharply—
about five percentage points.

The fact that we are increasingly buying on impulse
rather than on plan certainly suggests strongly that, as a
people, we do not think very carefully about how we
spend our money.

We are as unwise in *not* spending money as often as
in spending it. We put off buying enough life insurance
or an accident policy, or buying a few shares of a good
stock, or making needed repairs in time to the house or
the car, or having the whole family's teeth attended to,
or getting regular medical checkups. The consequences
of such failures to spend at the right time can be enormously expensive a few years hence.

The maxim "it's hard to spend money" applies to
business as well as to personal living. There are many
indications that more companies get into serious trouble
because *management* doesn't know how to spend properly
than because of inability to sell the company's products
or services.

So, BEAR IN MIND . . .

Earning money is hard enough. It's even harder to
spend wisely. But, wise spending is the easiest way to earn
money.

The money you earn from investments is taxed less
than the wages you receive from regular work.

Don't make the popular mistake of thinking your salary or wages are the only way you can earn money. Consider the many practical ways you can invest your funds—and let that money earn more money for you.

Spending isn't good—or bad. Unwise spending that exhausts your money on things you don't need is certainly bad. However, it is foolish to not spend on wise investment, necessary insurance, upkeep on your house and car, and other reasonable items.

Saving on unnecessary luxuries, and saving by careful shopping and planning of your needs, are additional ways to earn money which can be put to work for you.

Investment in industry is an established feature of American life. More than 20 million people own common stocks and, as shareholders in industry, they have a voice in management.

2. A Fair Day's Work

Most of us have to earn some money before we can spend it—or save it.

This is a rich country, but the boy or girl born to plenty is still a rarity. In the days before high inheritance taxes and very high income taxes, our fathers used to talk a lot about the iniquities of the idle rich—and with considerable justification. President Theodore Roosevelt, born rich himself, used to express his indignation forcibly about the intellectual banality, lack of public spirit and general uselessness of many of the rich society folk of his day.

President Franklin D. Roosevelt, also born rich, inveighed mightily and with considerable effect against the short-sighted views of people he called "economic royalists."

But the omnipresent tax-gatherer has worked a subtle change in the psychology of people of property. Educators have noticed many boys and girls from well-to-do families tend to have a sober respect for thrift nowadays. They may not have the capacity to create wealth that their hard-fisted forebearers had, but they do not have the inclination to throw away the Old Man's hard-gained money recklessly.

Young people from families in modest circumstances, on the other hand, tend to be wasteful with money once they start earning some, the educators and social workers have observed. They want to make up for the deprivations of their childhood. This is a dangerous attitude, a childish attitude—and it can lead to a great deal of trouble, to constant debt resulting from extravagant indulgence, to bickering between husband and wife, to broken marriages, and to children again raised in deprivation of physical comfort and parental love and lack of security.

It seems to me that a reasonable thrifty attitude toward money is certain to inculcate a reasonably thrifty attitude toward work, and that a habit of extravagance is more apt to make people slovenly about work than to make them good producers, good employees of good businessmen.

"A fair day's work for a fair day's pay," may seem to many of today's young people to be an old-fashioned idea, almost a "sucker play." And in some companies, it must be confessed, there is enough favoritism, enough miscarriage of justice, to give impressionable young folk that opinion.

The young man sees a fellow who "bird dogs" day after day get promoted over the hard worker because he dazzles the boss with flattery, or does him favors, or dates his homely daughter.

But this kind of opportunist has a heck of a good chance of being seen through completely by the boss before he is able to pull off a real coup. When that happens, he's finished and has to look for a new job.

On the other hand, determining from the start that you are going to sell your services in the same "value received" basis that you would expect if you were hiring people, will pay off in the long run—just as living all phases of your life by the time-honored golden rule does.

I don't know whether Benjamin Franklin's autobiography is still required reading in the grammar schools across the country or not. If you never had to read it, it will pay you to get it from the library. You can read it in two evenings and you will find it extremely interesting as well as instructive. The conditions under which Franklin lived and worked in New York, Philadelphia and London aren't much like ours, but the principles and precepts he learned the hard way are still valid.

To give a fair day's wage for a fair day's pay nowadays doesn't mean staying out of the union or licking the boss's hand. In many trades you can't stay out of the union even if you want to. Some companies are rather quick to promote a young man who serves as a union officer and who does a good job at it. "If he did well for the union, he'll do well for the company," the management reasons. "It shows he has wide interests, energy and courage."

Rather, to give a fair day's work for a fair day's pay means to have an industrious and studious attitude toward the job itself and an attitude of sober—but not sentimental —loyalty to the company or to your boss, unless he is the type of character who can't command anyone's loyalty.

The willingness to give a little more than the minimum time to the job before turning in an overtime slip is a good mark of the worker who wants to give a fair day's work for his pay. But don't break union rules and offend other workers by piling up many hours on a union job without turning in an overtime slip.

Sticking at it while on the job and refraining from wasting time in endless conversation is another way to be sure you're earning the day's pay honestly. And that does *not* mean working at breakneck speed; that will only make other people around you nervous and is likely to cause you to make costly mistakes.

Much more serious is the attitude of some young people today that a job should not entail much real work, interest, or responsibility. There was a gag greeting card on sale in shops a few months back that said, "I put in 40 hours in this dump—do you expect me to work too?"

Exasperated employers say they have encountered a discouraging number of people, youngsters and some in the prime of life, in recent years who seem to have exactly that attitude.

It's an attitude that will not let you learn how to make money—or how to spend it or save it.

The lackadaisical, unproductive worker doesn't realize how much harm he is doing to himself or to his fellow workers and his country. Unless the productivity and efficiency of workers keeps up reasonably with the improved technology of industry and commerce, the employer has a huge incentive to invest more and more money in machines and methods that reduce the number of workers.

And when the union leaders go up to negotiate for better wages and for more job-security provisions in the new contract, they have a tough time if they cannot show that productivity of the workers is at least keeping up with advances of technology.

In the small business that is not unionized, the lazy, nonproductive worker gets short shrift from the boss, or is miserably paid if he is kept on.

In the unionized trades and bigger businesses, the attempts of short-sighted workers and some short-sighted union leaders to limit productivity of the individual worker and to keep the payroll padded by varying degrees of featherbedding, run costs up substantially. But it is doubtful if union rules and featherbedding cost industry and commerce anywhere near as much as plain laziness and carelessness, failure of individuals to live up to what common honesty should dictate as normal or even minimum standards for a fair day's work.

This unwillingness of many people to work reasonably hard is a big cause of our inflationary spiral.

The automobile that sold for $850 in 1932 sells for $2,000 today. Unquestionably, much that goes into its higher price has little to do with ordinary labor costs. Yet, it is almost certain that if auto workers put out as much effort now as they did in 1932, that car would cost somewhat less—even at today's wage levels.

The effect of all this on our ability as a nation to export goods is considerable. And we are feeling it just when, for the first time in our national history, we have to be seriously concerned about what economists call our international balance of payments—the difference between what we spend abroad on imported goods, including vital raw materials, foreign aid and military expenditures— and how much we take in on our exports. We have had a substantial deficit in our balance of payments for a number of years.

Peoples of nations that live by exporting—the British, the Dutch, the Belgians, the Swiss, the West Germans and the Japanese, for examples—learned long ago that their labor had to keep up its productivity, or they would perish from the earth. The factory worker in these countries is unionized; he gets relatively low wages but high fringe benefits. His productivity traditionally was not as good as the American worker's, because the American worker was backed up by better machines, more modern plants and more efficient management techniques.

But now, to a considerable extent, the shoe is on the other foot. The European worker and sometimes even the Japanese worker has more modern machinery, and his company's management skill is every bit as good as the American's. So we can't afford lazy, inefficient workers in offices or factories any longer. And, being lazy and inefficient at work tends to make a man or a woman equally lazy and inefficient at home—and also likely to be very inefficient at spending money.

Even if I am crucified for it, I feel constrained to remark that television and frozen pre-packed dinners are the worst enemies to successful living ever devised. They waste more time keeping people from doing useful things and engaging in self-study and improvement and break up more homes than liquor or gambling.

How can a man hope to be respected by his wife and children if he degenerates into a slob sprawled all evening in front of the TV, lapping up one can of beer after another?

In studies of life in Suburbia, some of our leading clergymen and sociologists have been struck forcibly by the way the every-night television habit eats insidiously into the moral fiber of the nation. It is not so much the violence and general shoddiness of much of the programming as it is the pernicious habit of wasting so much time in a dream world. The theater and films—and even television—can bring great joy into our lives, but to spend nearly all of every evening in such cheap escapism is bound to be intellectually and morally debilitating.

So, BEAR IN MIND . . .

A healthy, sensible attitude towards money—and how to use it—should be a regular part of the education of children. A thrifty attitude towards money indicates an understanding that fair wages require, and deserve, fair labor.

Overspending can be a habit which leads to considerable grief inside the family circle. Often, people who were economically deprived as children unthinkingly try to make up for this by overspending—often for unnecessary things.

It makes good economic sense to work hard for the money you receive as wages. A profit-making company stays in business. Unions are an accepted feature of our American society and management respects leadership qualities in union members. Honesty requires your observance of both company and union rules.

3. What Does It Cost to Live?

There's an old gag to the effect that the cost of living invariably is five to ten dollars a week more than you earn—whether you make thirty bucks or a thousand.

But Uncle Sam's Bureau of Labor Statistics claims it really can measure the cost of living. Furthermore, statisticians claim that the personal income of Americans has gone up four times as fast, since World War II, as has the bare cost of living.

A variety of new taxes have been invented by the various governmental units to siphon off some of this money. And most of us divert other big chunks of it into insurance payments, educational fees, bigger home mortgages, bigger cars, and other things people did without before the war.

Still, many people don't know how much it should cost them to live, and the government's average figures are only the loosest sort of guidelines. They are based mainly on life in big cities, where it is easier for the various government information offices to check prices. The Bureau of Labor Statistics warns that its figures are in general somewhat high for small towns where rents may be cheap. But the fact that the cost of living in big cities is higher doesn't mean big-city folks are worse off than small-town people. Union scales and other salary scales are normally considerably higher in big cities, too.

The government figures show some rather surprising disparities in the basic cost of living among the big cities. It doesn't surprise us so much that, in 1963, it costs almost

24

$1,200 a year more for a family of four to live in Boston than in Houston—$6,790 against $5,606. After all, Boston has a cold climate, is highly industrialized, and is far from the nation's main sources of foods, fuel and raw materials. And wage scales are excellent in Boston.

But why is the cost of living in Los Angeles almost as high as in Boston, considering the West Coast city's mild climate and close proximity to the great farming regions? Obviously, it's because Southern California's climate puts premium costs on land and everything developed on the land.

Why is Chicago among the most expensive places to live in the country? And why is New York, in spite of its thousands of $1,000 a month luxury apartments, one of the cheaper big cities to live in—with a basic cost, for a family of four, of $6,352?

For New York the answer is simple—rent control and cheap transportation.

But rent is not by any means the sole determining factor in the geographical cost of living. The Bureau of Labor Statistics puts the average annual *food cost* for a family of four in Atlanta at $1,571; in New York, it is 25 per cent more, $1,975.

Nor are salaries always gauged to the regional cost of living. Pay scales in the high-cost cities of the Pacific Coast are lower than in Boston, New York or Chicago. Nor are all small towns cheap. The mass movement of people from the big cities to nearby small towns since World War II has run land prices sky high in many of these suburban areas and has increased their tax rates enormously.

So, when a young couple decide where to locate, if they have a choice in the matter and aren't compelled to settle in the one place where the husband can find a good job or where both can work, they should consider the *cost of living differentials*. They can mean quite a lot.

Even if they are high for smaller towns, the Bureau of

Labor Statistics averages are unrealistically low for a safe total cost-of-living estimate anywhere in the United States. In the first place, they do not normally include enough for shelter by at least $20 a month. That's because they are based on average rents, including those in the worst slums. Nor do they generally allow enough for *taxes and insurance*. Remember that a family of four has a federal income tax exemption of $2,400 and a standard deduction of $1,000 or less. The rest of the income is taxable at 16 per cent and up.

But the biggest reason the Bureau of Labor Statistics estimates seem to me to be too low for a safe standard of living is that they do not take into account the amount of *interest and finance charges* the average family must pay these days. Moreover, as we shall see later, every family should save 3 to 10 per cent of its gross income—not the net income—in cash, on top of what is saved by way of life insurance premiums and principal payments on a home mortgage. Taking all these things into consideration, it seems to me that a reasonable safe standard of living must be about 25 per cent above the estimates of the Bureau of Labor Statistics. When the Bureau says the basic cost of living for a family of four—two school age children and the parents—in Baltimore is a virtually level $6,000, then I suggest a more realistic level is $7,500 or $147.50 a week; that's gross pay, not take-home pay.

Of course, a couple with two very small children can live more cheaply; and millions of couples manage to raise two children on $5,000 a year or less in many parts of the country. But they do so either because of very special circumstances, or at great sacrifice, or they go into serious debt.

What I am driving at is that many people ought to have a more *realistic* idea of what it costs to live in decent circumstances in these days. And let us concede right now that even the $7,500 figure is not going to leave room for any extravagances for a family of four living in Baltimore. If more couples faced the facts before assuming heavy obligations they have little chance of carrying, we would have fewer broken homes and not nearly so many personal "grasshopper" bankruptcies in this country.

What it costs you individually to live, and how you will meet that cost and earn more besides, will depend to a great extent on whether you think about *when to do what,* or just drift along and meet, or try to meet, each need and each crisis as it comes along or act on impulse.

Acting on impulse can be just as dangerous as procrastinating. It will make you invest money in certain things long before you really need them or can get the most out of them. On big items, like a house or an expensive car, you have mortgaged your future for several years by an unwise investment—when opportunity does strike, you haven't the money to take advantage.

The consequences of drifting and not trying to foresee any of your future needs are obvious. It isn't enough just to resolve not to drift; *you've got to make a plan for the future,* put it down on paper, have it clearly understood by your wife and by your children, then stick to it.

So, BEAR IN MIND . . .

Your cost of living, and how much you should spend for the things you need, cannot be estimated by any simple rule. Each expenditure should be carefully planned in terms of your income and all your other expenses. Remember, life today is more complex—and more things are considered necessities—than years ago.

Wages vary in different areas of the country, as do living expenses. But . . . low wages can be the rule in some high-living-cost areas. This is something to consider when you plan to move.

The cost of heating your home is a big item—if you

live in the northern portion of our country. Don't forget this, if you are thinking of a change of scene.

The government cost-of-living figures provided by the Bureau of Labor Statistics are carefully compiled—but, to be realistic, add about 25 per cent to the government figures, if you use them.

You must plan your spending. The more pleasant and satisfying life becomes, the more complex it must be. Still, it only requires a little forethought and planning to solve this problem.

4. Squandermania

It's amazing how many people squander money buying things they don't need, can't use and don't really want.

Squandermania is a neurosis that affects a lot of people. Sometimes its results are astonishing. I know of a successful author who was ruined financially by marrying a beautiful actress who had this disease. If he needed a new black tie to wear with his tuxedo, she would call the most expensive shop on Fifth Avenue and order two dozen black ties, the fanciest ones made. If they happened to be out at Southampton at the moment, she would have them sent by messenger.

After the divorce, the author married a much more frugal lady who set about trying to salvage something from his tangled finances. She found his home in suburban New York and his Southhampton summer home stuffed from basement to attic with unopened boxes of merchandise the ex-wife had bought on impulse in Europe, Florida, Boston, New York and California.

There was a collection of books on occult philosophy on which some thousands of dollars had been squandered, yet they had never been read. There were suits, the $200 kind, ordered in half-dozen lots and never worn. The lady had squandered money on furnishings and paintings and plants for the grounds in the same way. On one occasion, the author drove home to Southhampton from a week's trip to New York. Arriving after dark, he was amazed to find his garage had disappeared and a new rose garden had taken its place. His wife had spent several thousand dollars

29

to have a contractor move the garage out of sight and transplant full-grown blooming rosebushes from a nursery.

Few of us have the chance to indulge in squandermania on such a scale, but many people do mortgage their own future and frustrate their savings programs by wasteful buying. They do so because they don't learn how to buy things when they are young.

Europeans used to say the average American housewife wasted enough food to support a European family. Doubtless, this was an exaggeration and, nowadays, the food processors have found so many new ways to process and package foods that there is much less *waste*. A lot of this processing is expensive, but it saves money in the long run because spoilage is largely eliminated. Moreover, the fact that the food is so easily prepared frees many housewives so that they can hold down part-time or even full-time jobs and add to the family income. Still, if you find your garbage pail is plumb full for every collection, there is a good chance you are overbuying at the supermarket and you are preparing too generously for each meal. Consider the matter carefully and start cutting down a little on portions.

Many families probably waste money on food simply by *overeating*. The meals contain too many calories for optimum health. The housewife who doesn't take the trouble to buy a book on balanced diet or to get one from the library and study it is wasting money as well as gambling with her family's health. I'm not going to try to discuss balanced diet, but just one example of how much money can be saved by careful variation of the family's meals will suffice—some delicious and nutritious varieties of fish cost as little as 20 cents a pound at the butcher shop against 75 cents and up for beef.

And there's no doubt that *an over-rich* diet is a prime factor in our high rate of cardio-vascular and other diseases that weaken the body's organs and tissues. By overeating or living on too rich a diet, you are squandering money to shorten your life.

The cost of alcoholism is something everybody knows about, but have you considered the high cost of too much social drinking or too much smoking? *Liquor and tobacco* are the most heavily taxed luxuries we consume. Excessive social drinking is so expensive that even if no alcoholism problem develops in the family, the burdensome cost can be destructive to the family's economic hopes.

There are too many ways to squander money even to try to list them in a book like this. The point is to learn, and to teach the children, to control impulse spending. Buy things only because you need them or will derive a considerable and substantial satisfaction from having them, *not because they appeal to you at the moment.*

If you cultivate this habit, you are much less likely to end up with a car or a boat that is too big and expensive for you, with a house and lawn too big to take care of, and closets crammed with clothing you've worn only once and possibly have become too stout to wear.

Next to squandermania, *careless shopping* eats into the family income most heavily. There is an astonishing variation in the prices asked for standard merchandise in different kinds of stores and under different brand names.

Where is the best place to shop, a department store, a specialty shop or a discount store? It's a hard question to answer with a generalization, but, on balance, the department stores will score high, if for no other reason than because they have enormous selections and a big department store covers the whole price range of merchandise. You can get a $22 suit or a $3.98 dress in the basement or a $100 suit or a $150 dress in the high-fashion departments upstairs—and all under the same roof. If department store prices are higher than discount store prices, and specialty store prices are a little higher still, it's because of the service they give you and, above all, because of the exchange privileges. The cost of exchanges in women's garments is enormous, but many women will not buy unless they can take a dress back if they don't like it after they get home with it.

Many young people find buying extremely perplexing and difficult simply because they are inexperienced. They do not know much about the merits of different materials in garments, the merits of different designs in appliances and household devices. The conflicting advertising claims only serve to confuse them more. The mere appearance or feel of a piece of merchandise, to their inexperienced eyes, in no way seems to explain or justify the substantial difference in price between it and another item that looks much like it. How can you find out?

You can ask the clerk, of course. He will give you an answer, but the chances of his really knowing the facts are not nearly so great as they used to be. Sales clerks are no longer expected to know their stock as they were before World War II. In fact many stores use nearly all part-time sales help.

Of course you can find books in the library about practically every kind of merchandise, and they will give you sound factual information. The trouble is, the merchandise isn't marked in the stores with labels that will enable you to tell quickly just what it is made of or how it is made. It is brand marked. If it's a national brand that you know, that alone tells you quite a bit. But there are many thousands of national brands and advertising experts admit only a handful of them are really widely known. Besides, according to authoritative firms in New York that do the buying for big department stores, the trend to private brands is growing in retail trade and the private brand is, generally speaking, sold a little more cheaply than the national brand. Often the private brand merchandise is identical to the national brand. Today, a manufacturer of anything from hosiery to large appliances must have big volume at all costs. If he can't sell enough of his output under his own brand name, he is forced to sell the identical product, unbranded, to stores and groups of stores that put their own brand name on it and sell it a little cheaper.

One source of unbiased judgment on the merits of competing brands, both national and private, in all kinds of merchandise is the magazine *Consumer Reports,* which can be subscribed to or bought on newsstands in most cities. Consumers Union, which publishes the magazine, buys merchandise and tests it, then publishes the results, giving brand names and prices and saying which it considers the better buys. Occasionally, you hear of a manufacturer grumbling about the verdict on his products in *Consumer Reports,* but the outfit has been in business several decades now and has a high reputation for hewing to the line and letting the chips fall where they will.

So, in one way or another, *you must take the trouble to learn about merchandise* and not buy it blindly nor swallow advertising claims whole, if you are not going to waste money. Advertising is rarely deliberately false or highly exaggerated. But no manufacturer is obligated to tell you that his competitor has a lower overhead than he has and can undersell him as a result, or that another competitor has a patent on a process that gives his product a definite edge in value.

So, bear in mind . . .

Good buying habits are one element of thrift. If a policy of careful shopping is instilled in the child, the adult benefits. But, it's never too late to learn—and it pays!

Good buying habits relate to everything you do. One example is planning your food requirements for *each* meal for sensible portions of good and economical food. Over-eating is often a sign of poor planning that resulted in oversupply. An overrich diet is another unhealthy and expensive practice.

Watch your taxes. Liquor and tobacco are luxuries—and they are very heavily taxed.

Think ahead when you buy. Impulse buying is a double evil—you spend on things you don't really desire or need, and you often pay more if you buy on impulse than you would if you took the time to shop around. This applies to your regular purchases, too. Different shops sell the same merchandise, often under different brand names, at dissimilar prices. You can save by careful shopping.

Learn how to shop. Know what you buy by studying *Consumer Reports,* government bulletins, and other impartial sources. Also, take the trouble to examine your purchases carefully—before you buy.

Buying is an art.

5. To Save Is to Save

The most important thing about spending your money is to not spend all of it.

The habit of saving should be taught to children early, and they should be taught the difference between saving and hoarding. *Saving means putting money aside to be used; hoarding means just putting it aside.*

People hoard in obedience to fear or to some morbid compulsion. People save so they will have some money when there's an illness, when the TV picture tube or the transmission in the car suddenly goes out, or if Pop gets held up and relieved of his wallet, or for some other emergency.

Even better, people save to accumulate the down payment on a house or a car, to buy a diamond ring or a boat, or to get a cash stake with which to start a planned investment program.

To illustrate the difference between saving and hoarding, let's look at a family of savers suddenly confronted with an emergency requiring $200. The family has been in the habit of putting $25 a month in their savings account. When the emergency occurs, there is no panic— the $200 is withdrawn from the savings bank to pay the emergency bill; *but that month, as every month, another $25 deposit is made.* Why should there be any panic over the dent in the savings account? That's what the money was saved for. Instead, there's satisfaction that a loan didn't have to be taken to meet the emergency.

Under the same circumstances the hoarder would panic

because of the emergency; even if he had many times $200 in the bank, he would try desperately to think of some way to avoid drawing it out and paying. If it is a medical emergency, the hoarder might risk his health or even his life by trying to get by without the expensive treatment. If the emergency is for repairs to the house or the car, he will try to get the cheapest, makeshift job possible—and will agonize over the cost of *that*.

We all have seen stories in the papers from time to time about people who destroyed themselves by the hoarding mania—dying in hovels of malnutrition when they had thousands of dollars in bank accounts or stashed away in old tin cans.

That has nothing to do with sensible saving.

It's also advisable to know the difference between saving and investing. Because most people invest their savings in some manner, they are likely to get the two ideas mixed up.

Saving is setting money aside for use, as we have seen. *Investing is putting money to work* to earn more money. We are saving even if we only keep pennies in a piggybank so long as we intend ultimately to make use of them and are not merely hoarding them—but when we accumulate enough pennies to put them in a savings bank so they will draw a little interest, we are investing them.

Putting money in a savings bank account is investing and saving at the same time—because savings accounts are so safe that there is virtually no risk involved.

But *when we buy stocks or bonds* with our savings, we no longer can truly be said to be saving because we are *risking our money to make it grow*. Technically, we are no longer saving it—that is, keeping it safe.

Of course, practically speaking, the risks in many investments nowadays are slight, so we often can feel we are getting the benefits of both a savings program and an investment program from the same deal. But technically, that isn't the case. There is no such thing as a risk-free investment, and the bigger promise an investment has, the bigger the element of risk it has, as a general rule, although this is far from an absolute law.

The easiest way to save and invest at the same time is by having the boss make weekly deductions from your paycheck to buy Series E Treasury Savings Bonds. This involves no strain on your part and no self-discipline, and the bonds are easy to cash when emergencies come.

But the 3 per cent return on your money isn't much of an investment. Almost any other small savings investment plan will pay you more.

In this country, about the highest interest on ordinary savings deposits is paid by *savings and loan associations,* which borrow savings from the public to lend back in residential mortgages. Their interest rates to savers (which technically are dividend rates since in most states your deposit buys a share in the association's stock) vary from state to state and from time to time. Where the demand for mortgage money is greatest and mortgage interest is highest, naturally the dividend on S&L shares is highest. Right now that is in California, where many S&L's are paying as much as 4.85 per cent.

The California S&L's advertise in many cities for deposits by mail, and even appoint brokerage offices as their deposit agents in New York and some other big cities to accept deposits on small commissions.

The savings and loan association has the right to change its interest rates on your shares as market conditions alter. Technically, the S&L can require you to give 30 days notice before cashing in your shares and withdrawing your savings. But the Savings Association League of New York advises that, in practice, this rule is nearly always waived and usually you can cash in S&L shares almost as easily as drawing your money from a bank.

Dividends on S&L deposits (or shares) are federally insured up to $10,000. And the dividend or interest nearly always is compounded quarterly at the annual rate. The early growth of your savings on compound interest may not sound astonishing, but in later years the results are good. At the 4 per cent annual rate prevailing in the East now, a deposit of $20 a month in a savings and loan association for 10 years would earn $552.74 on total deposits of $2,400.

Regular savings banks and the savings departments of commercial banks also pay compound interest on savings deposits, but usually at rates slightly under those of the S&L's.

The next question is, how much you should save? The table most frequently used by savings banks to advise people starts with 3 per cent of your income for earnings up to $75 a week and rises by degrees to 10 per cent of an income of $250 a week or more. You may wish to know whether the amortization portion of the monthly mortgage payment on your house is savings. Definitely, it is savings, but it shouldn't be counted in the 3 to 10 per cent recommended level. That level is calculated mainly on the basis of families that pay rent.

The savings you gain by buying your own house are extra and should be kept extra. And, of course, the part that goes for amortization in monthly payments on your car or television set is not savings; it may be an investment of sorts, but more likely it is simply a purchase of something being consumed.

Are life insurance premiums savings? And do you need to save cash if you invest heavily in life insurance? As a life insurance man, I naturally am proud of the way life insurance enables people, who otherwise would save nothing, to save for the future. But, candidly, life insurance primarily is risk protection and provision for your survivors. *Life insurance is a much better buy as straight protection than as a means of saving.* So you must save cash no matter how much or what kind of life insurance you carry.

So, BEAR IN MIND . . .

Saving means putting money aside for future use; hoarding is putting money aside—and keeping it out of circulation. Saving is a sign of common sense; hoarding is often a sign of unhealthy thinking.

It is all right to use your savings when you need them, but continue to save regularly even when you draw from your funds.

Investing means putting money to work for you. It is one possible goal for the money you *save.*

Treasury savings bonds are the easiest way to save— but this method is not very profitable.

Some savings and loan associations pay substantial interest. Nevertheless, in return for the simplicity and security of this form of saving, you accept a smaller return than is available to you elsewhere.

Insurance is insurance; saving and investing are different things and should be kept apart from your insurance needs.

6. Life Insurance—It's Wonderful

The bridegroom should have a substantial life insurance policy before he buys the wedding ring; it's more important. If he doesn't buy life insurance before the wedding, there is far too much chance that it will be put off until after the first baby is born, and I have seen many a man die or be killed during his wife's first pregnancy, leaving her destitute.

Generally, *people should start buying life insurance when they begin to need it,* for life insurance, as we've said before, is protection. It is *not* an ideal way to save even though, as we shall see, it is about the only way the average American can create an estate for his family under present conditions. The only reason for buying life insurance before you require the protection for dependents, is to protect your insurability. That, to my mind, is the only sensible reason for ever insuring the lives of children.

In general, *I don't believe in insuring the lives of children.* It simply spends money that is better spent in insuring the life of the breadwinner. Fifty years ago, when child mortality was around 50 per cent, the big life insurance companies rightly persuaded families to buy some insurance on children because funeral expenses of children were a recurrent burden to many families, particularly immigrant families. But children don't die often nowadays and, when they do, their funeral expenses are not an unbearable burden on the family.

The idea that buying an insurance policy for a child is a great bargain (because the rates are relatively low at that age), is not true. The number of years for which the premium will have to be paid before any collection is made on the policy more than offsets the low rate.

If the family is well-to-do and has plenty of insurance on the breadwinner, insuring the lives of the children for substantial amounts may then be a good hedge against the risk that the children will have health problems and be unable to get insurance in adulthood. I think this is the only sound reason for insuring the lives of children. I have encountered families paying out huge monthly sums in life insurance premiums and only 20 per cent of the amount was in insurance on the breadwinner. In most such cases it seemed to me that 75 per cent of what they were spending was wasted and the death of the breadwinner was certain to mean financial disaster for the family.

If there are two breadwinners in the family, circumstances may indicate insuring both heavily. But usually it is best for the average family to put all the life insurance on the life of the father. That is where the big risk is, and life insurance is protection against risk. *A widow or single woman may need as much life insurance as a man—if she has dependents and an estate problem.*

The average American family has about $12,500 in life insurance protection. That is only one-and-a-half years income for the family. For a long time, life insurance men have known that the average amount of insurance carried is grossly inadequate. They now recommend that the average family have life insurance policies equal to at least four times the annual income. The truth of the matter is that for many, perhaps for the majority of families, if the insurance is properly bought, forty or fifty thousand dollars of insurance, or even one hundred thousand dollars worth, does not cost much more than the average amount of $12,500.

Let's take the family (mentioned in Chapter Three)

living in Baltimore on $7,500 a year. Joe Baltimore, as we shall call him, is 32 years old. He has a $10,000 twenty-year endowment policy in the X,Y,Z Life Insurance Company, a little over a year old, which costs him $531 a year. But if Joe Baltimore went to a first-class life insurance agent, he would discover that for his $531 a year he could buy $104,800 in life insurance from the ABC Life Insurance Company.

It would work this way. The agent would sell out the endowment policy, buy Joe a $10,000 ordinary life policy and $94,800 worth of decreasing term insurance. On Joe's death this could pay his widow during the important years of the family's life either $104,800 in cash or $10,000 in cash and $500 a month for 20 years.

Now, granted this policy would diminish in value over the years and would protect Joe's family only during the years the children were growing up, except for the $10,000 ordinary life, it would leave them with the problem of rearranging his life insurance after the children are grown. But it *would* create an immediate estate for his family of $104,800, and would give him peace of mind during the hurly burly years of his life.

Protection is what Joe wanted from his insurance and he will be getting it. On the other hand, with his present endowment policy, if he dies, his wife gets $10,000, and, if he survives, he can cash it in for the same amount after 20 years.

As a matter of fact, $531 is probably considerably more than Joe ought to be spending on life insurance premiums on his income. For $275 a year, he could get $5,000 in straight life and $47,500 in decreasing term insurance protection, and in this way create for himself an immediate estate of $52,400 which would give his wife a twenty-year income of $250 a month and $5,000 in cash.

Have you ever stopped to think that when you buy

$100,000 worth of automobile liability insurance, you are, in effect, insuring the life of some chap you don't know and protecting his wife to the tune of $100,000—while you may have but $12,500 in life insurance protection for your own wife?

Put another way, does it make sense to insure mere physical property for 80 per cent of its value, and to insure *your own life* for only 2 to 10 per cent of your minimum expectable life earnings as measured by your present salary?

Let's take Joe Baltimore's case again. He's 32 and has a further life expectancy of 38 years, productive years, if you will. Doesn't it stand to reason that his human-life value should be at least his present income of $7,500 multiplied by his 38 years of life expectancy? This total of $285,000 is really what he is worth to his family—if you can measure it in money. Why, therefore, does the average chap in similar circumstances claim he is worth more dead than alive because he has a mere $10,000 in life insurance protection?

Diminishing term policies have only been available for about the past 15 years. They are still not very well known and we are not likely to hear about them. That brings up the question of from whom one should buy life insurance.

As a life insurance man, I can tell you that the professional agent or broker makes his living from the policyholder rather than from the company. The size of his income is directly related to his knowledge and integrity and how he advises his clients. And only he has the expert knowledge of all types of insurance necessary to give you the best program. In other words, your insurance broker or agent serves you as your doctor does and deserves your confidence in the same way.

The diminishing term insurance, in addition to providing maximum protection at minimum premium cost during the period the family is growing, also usually can be obtained on a basis that makes it convertible into straight life insurance without further physical examination at additional premium cost.

The importance of having a large amount of term insurance that is convertible without further physical examination cannot be overemphasized. Recently a client of mine had a rather large business proposition offered to him that required his life to be insured for $100,000. As it turned out, when he was examined for this business policy, he was turned down by the insurance company doctors because of high blood pressure. The day was saved when I pointed out to him that three years before, I had added to his life insurance program $150,000 of five year renewable and convertible term insurance. This enabled him to buy into this successful corporation because the insurance was available that was required, and from all indications, he can look forward to a very successful business.

When I said that the only way to create an estate under present conditions for most families is their life insurance, perhaps I aroused some skepticism. But how could your grandfather have possibly created an estate of $104,800 at age 32 without suddenly increasing his income or perhaps winning the Irish Sweepstakes? Joe Baltimore can do it through life insurance.

However, this does create a misunderstanding on the part of some people. They confuse creating an estate with saving, and they continue to believe that life insurance is such a fine way to save that it isn't necessary to save money. As we pointed out in the last chapter, this is totally untrue.

The idea of buying life insurance when you can get it, instead of when you need it desperately, applies to adults as well as to children. I have seen many cases of people who put off buying life insurance until some sudden change in their health made it impossible for them to get it. Many people simply do not realize when they need life insurance. In my own experience, I have seen more than one tragedy caused by this failure. Some years ago I suggested $10,000 worth of partnership life to each of two partners in a garage where I kept my car. One partner bought $10,000 personal life and wanted to buy the partnership policy but he couldn't persuade the other chap to buy. In six months, Ed, the partner who wanted to buy the partnership policy, was dead. Tom did not get any insurance on his partner's life and could not get the cash to pay Ed's widow a fair price for Ed's interest in the business. Contrast this with two other clients of mine, successful accountants, who took out $50,000 in partnership insurance. In less than a year, the younger partner, aged only 30, was dead from leukemia but no financial hardship resulted.

I have seen many other cases. A doctor in New York City, with a very large and substantial practice, called me in for a consultation. I found him terribly underinsured. Based on his current income, I worked out a program that would have cost him $2,000 in premiums. He refused to buy it, saying he preferred to spend it on his teen-age children's education. In less than a year the doctor dropped dead. In spite of the high income from his practice, the doctor's estate was bankrupt, his children did not get to college, and the widow was left almost destitute.

The ladies are not going to like this, but I think they are the main cause of inadequate life insurance protection. The husband usually is willing to buy more life insurance protection but the wife wants to spend the money on a better house, more clothes and other current expenditures. *Some women even have an old-fashioned, morbid dread of life insurance.* They don't want to talk about it at all, think it unlucky to talk about it. The irony of it is that the day the husband dies the wife's attitude changes. I have never known a widow who thought her husband had too much insurance.

I mentioned a doctor a minute ago. I sold another doctor a $120,000 policy, and in less than three years, he died, comparatively young. His children went to college and his widow has no financial worries at all. The doctors say themselves they have the lowest life expectancies of any of the professions. Yet surprisingly, many of them don't get around to buying enough life insurance.

Life insurance—it's wonderful. In my twenty year business career I have seen untold misery and destitution because "tomorrow" was always time enough to talk about the dollars our loved ones would need. Often "tomorrow" never comes. I have also seen widows and children still able to keep their heads high after the death of the breadwinner because he had the foresight to protect them "just in case." I have seen businesses fail under the weight of a dead uninsured partner. I have also seen others continue and prosper for the benefit of the survivors of the business as well as the estate, because of adequate financial planning in advance.

Now, a word of caution about the *settlement options* in life insurance contracts. Many life insurance companies develop salesmen who profess to have an ability to plan your estate for you. In pursuing this clairvoyant role they may ask you to sign settlement options many years in advance, such as deciding that it will be wiser for your wife to get the insurance in monthly installments instead of a lump sum. The trouble with that is that it can backfire very badly. For example, suppose in his wisdom, John Doe, listening to the sage advice of a salesman, decides it will be risky to let his wife Mary have control of $20,000 all at once, and he signs a settlement option that she is to be paid so much a month. But, at the time John dies, Mary may be destitute and John may have left many debts. The small monthly payments may even be earmarked in the settlement option for certain definite purposes such as educating the children.

There is no legal way to revoke these options in a will or after the death of the policyholder. The insurance company is obliged by law to carry them out no matter how much hardship is on the widow. The insurance company may even be making a little money in interest on invested funds of the policy, which it certainly does not want to do at the widow's expense. Therefore, options usually should be left for a later settlement. If there is a soundly drawn will, it is often advisable to have the bread-winner's insurance made payable to his estate in order to provide for various contingencies. But if there's not a soundly drawn will, having insurance made payable to the estate is very dangerous. Then creditors may take the proceeds of the policy away from the widow, or other heirs may do so. The reason for making a policy payable to the estate is only so that the proceeds can be disposed of in the will. A specific beneficiary cannot be changed by will, only by action of the policyholder during his lifetime.

The annuity is one of the oldest forms of insurance and is still written by nearly all life insurance companies. It means that after you have paid in a certain sum, the company hereafter guarantees to pay you a regular monthly or quarterly sum for the rest of your life. The ancient Romans invented the annuity and it remained popular for centuries, long before modern life insurance was dreamed of.

In the 18th and 19th centuries, and even in the first thirty years of this century, when currencies were very stable and taxes very low, annuities made a lot of sense and many people managed to live comfortably on them in their declining years. *Today, the annuity simply is too expensive and too vulnerable to inflation and other rapidly changing conditions to make it a sound investment or much protection.*

So, BEAR IN MIND . . .

Buy life insurance as soon as you need it. If you put off buying insurance your eligibility may change because of your medical record.

There is no point to insuring the lives of children today. The place for heavy insurance is on the life of the family's breadwinner.

Life insurance is not expensive if it is properly selected.

Buy your life insurance from a professional insurance man. This is a complex subject and poor advice can be costly.

Life insurance is a poor way to save—but you can use it to build an estate.

Some wives have a foolish, superstitious dread of life insurance. This attitude is unfair to themselves and to their children.

Settlement options are tricky, and it is best to leave them open.

A soundly drawn will is necessary in any case; and, if you have one you can make your insurance payable to your estate.

Annuity plans are a poor form of life insurance.

7. Long Live Credit!

Life without credit would be horrid.

Life with too much credit is worse than horrid—it's a nightmare. In many countries, millions of people live out their whole lives in debt-slavery because of the high cost of credit. This is particularly true in Latin America and in South European and Asiatic countries where the peasantry still live on huge feudal estates, pay exorbitant rents, and never get out of debt. We've had some of that sort of thing in the United States within the memory of many living Americans: the coal miner who never succeeded in completely paying off the bill at the company store, the sharecropper who never quite managed to balance his account with the plantation owner or with the "furnish merchant."

But, *the sensible expansion* of credit in our industrial civilization has done a great deal to make life pleasant and meaningful and to give hope of advancement to millions who, in past times, existed like dull clods.

The sensible expansion of credit can occur only when the cost of credit is reduced greatly. And that is what has happened in the United States in the past century, most particularly in the past fifty years.

Credit always costs. Whenever you say "Charge it!" you are paying something more, in one way or another, than you would pay for the same item or service in cash. More than half the time the additional sum you pay in order to "charge it" is a good investment. For it is credit that makes it possible for the American working man or the little merchant or the schoolteacher to own a home, keep an automobile, be protected by all forms of insurance, have an electric refrigerator, a television receiver, an air conditioner, to not live in fear of hospital and medical expense, to dress decently, and to have a reasonable hope of sending his kids to college.

Because the cost of credit has been so greatly reduced and has been extended to so many people in our time, far too many young people and older people (who ought to know better) take credit too much for granted and don't inform themselves about how much it costs, and how many different kinds of credit there are, and how to select the ones that are best for particular needs.

Although the cost of credit is about the best buy of anything you purchase—it still is not cheap. For example, the credit cost of buying a house runs from a minimum of 50 per cent of the purchase price, for a short mortgage and a big downpayment, to 85 percent of the purchase price for a long mortgage and a small down payment. The cost of credit to buy an automobile can run to 20 per cent of the purchase price. These are the legitimate costs of sound and honest credit plans. If you fall into the hands of an unscrupulous loan shark, as the illiterate frequently do, you can end up paying $300 in credit costs to buy a $500 jalopy!

So one of the hardest ways of all to spend money wisely is to spend it for credit. *You must inform yourself about the different kinds of credit and what they cost.* It doesn't really take a head for figures, but you need to know the principles involved.

In our day of free and easy credit, when an improvident debtor can escape his obligations without any terrible stigma by filing a "grasshopper" bankruptcy petition in Federal Court, many forget or never have realized how harshly society has dealt in the past with people who abused credit.

In the ancient world interest rates were extremely high and the defaulting debtor paid a terrible penalty. If his property could not satisfy the claims of his creditors, his children, his wife and, finally, the debtor himself were sold in the public market into slavery. Nor was there any mitigating element of humanity in the laws and customs. Gently nurtured women and girls were ruthlessly sold to brothel keepers to pay the debt of husband and father. Sons of noblemen were sold into the most degrading and killing slavery. A ruined young nobleman in Rome might find himself overnight become a galley slave doomed to work himself to death in a few months under the lash at the oar, or even sold to some impresario staging a vast show in the amphitheater in which hundreds of slaves would be slaughtered by gladiators and wild beasts to make a spectacle for the mob.

It is probable that these horrible practices of rapacious Roman moneylenders and the cruel Roman law gave rise to the totally illogical prejudice which led the Church for more than one thousand years to forbid any Christian to lend money at interest. Where it was observed, this religious prohibition naturally had a terribly depressing effect on commerce and industry. But in general it was flouted in ingenious ways. The most usual way was for the Jewish community to undertake all money lending operations. Christian noblemen and merchants often were silent partners, putting up part of the capital and giving the Jewish bankers the protection of their military vassals. The barons thus avoided the Church's ban on lending money at interest, but shared handsomely in the profits. Sometimes, they even obtained Church funds for the business. The discounted loan (in which the interest is extracted *before* the money is handed over) was invented during these times, according to some historians, or at least it gained great currency. A discounted note need not show interest had been charged. Even so, throughout this period even kings dared not openly lend money at interest in Christendom. And every now and then in a moment of sadly mistaken zeal, a God-fearing court would burn some poor Jewish banker at the stake for lending money at interest!

By the end of the 15th century, interest on business and government loans, and even for such personal purposes as building a home, had won the sanction of the Church. In the immediately following centuries, Christians got into banking in a big way. But the stigma attached to borrowing money for personal purposes, as distinguished from business, continued. Debtors who couldn't pay were sent to prison or sold as indentured bond servants until about 1830 in Europe, and until the adoption of our Constitution on this side of the Atlantic.

In much of Europe and particularly in England there still is a stigma against borrowing money for personal purposes. And even in this country it still is possible to be sent to jail for some kinds of debt—failure to pay alimony, contempt of court for willful evasion of taxes, evasion of a hotel or board bill, for example. In general, in this country, we long ago espoused the sensible view that personal or consumer credit is every bit as beneficial to society as is business and government credit.

Economists and bankers classify credit in many ways but, for our purpose, *there are three main kinds of credit —business, mortgage and consumer.* Business credit is how your boss gets the money to run his business while waiting for the checks to come in from the customers. It consists primarily of ordinary short-term loans at the bank, long-term bonds or debentures he sells privately or through a stockbrokers' underwriting team to raise money for buying new machines or expanding the firm, and open-account credit extended to him by manufacturers and distributors on raw materials and supplies.

There are many other kinds of business credit: stockbrokers' margin accounts that enable one to buy stocks by putting up only about half the price in cash, loans from banks on securities or other collateral, and there are the loans obtained from such special institutions as factoring houses and commercial finance companies. Factors and commercial finance houses make comparatively risky loans to business at relatively high interest rates—12, 15 or even 20 per cent a year. A business that has to resort to such loans often, is in trouble; on the other hand, the commercial finance companies often provide skilled management help along with their loans that helps an ailing company get well.

Mortgage credit is the oldest and most respectable form of credit and is understood by the most people. We'll have a special chapter about it.

Consumer credit is the newest form of credit, the most diversified, the most expensive, and it possibly does the most to make life agreeable and to influence the short term rise and fall of the national economy. *It is expensive because it is retail credit.* The largest consumer loan would probably be for a $5,000 car, the smallest, a $50 personal loan or a $30 installment account.

It costs a bank or a finance company as much or more to make the investigation, conduct the interview, write up the paperwork, and collect the small installments on one of these little loans than it does to lend a couple of million dollars to a large corporation. That's the first reason consumer credit is expensive.

The second reason is that consumer credit is riskier than business credit. Many, perhaps most, of the loans are made to people who live from one paycheck to the next, have very small savings and who will have to use these savings for food purchases in case of unemployment or other serious trouble. The lender must collect interest and fees big enough to provide for these contingencies.

So, BEAR IN MIND . . .

Credit, alone, is a meaningless term. What we must look for is credit at a sensible price.

Credit always costs you money. Charge plans, credit cards, and open accounts are not exceptions to this rule.

There are many kinds of credit which may be useful to you. Study the forms that are available and select the one you will use.

Credit can account for 50% to 80% of the total cost of a house bought on time. It can take up to 20% of the money you spend for a car—and much more if you buy from a sharpie.

The different kinds of credit vary widely in cost—study them. Business, mortgage and consumer credit have their uses, and their prices.

8. How to Have Good Credit

When you go to a bank to ask for a loan, you are given a form to fill out that asks a lot of searching questions. You can tell by looking at the form that the bank is strict about loans.

But stores that extend credit on various plans, and automobile dealers, ask very little about you when you apply for credit. Why is this?

The answer is that banks generally prefer to do most of their own investigating, and they get a good start on the job in the first interview. The man at the bank isn't selling any merchandise at the same time; he doesn't have to lean over backward to make you feel happy and contented.

The dealers or store people, on the other hand, want above all to make you feel welcome. Even if they find they can't extend you credit, they hope you'll keep on buying from them—for cash. So they do their investigating unobtrusively, largely through credit bureaus or your bank references.

Some firms are very careless about credit investigations; sooner or later they get in trouble as a result.

But, never imagine because one store doesn't take the trouble to check up on what you tell them in a credit interview that others won't. Eight or nine of any ten given stores are very careful about checking up on applicants for credit.

That points up the first rule in getting a good credit standing: Never tell a lie in filling out a credit application.

Particularly, don't withhold information about other out-standing debts. The bank or store will find out about them. There are more than 2,000 retail credit bureaus in the United States that exchange information. In addition, many industries have special credit networks which exchange information about people.

These firms not only compare credit ratings, they watch bankruptcy, civil, criminal and police court records, and note items about people in the newspapers that have a bearing on their credit.

In business credit, a firm is rated largely on how much money it has—and how promptly it pays its bills.

In personal credit, these also are the two prime criteria; however, the question of how much money you have is not quite so important. Your personal reputation, your habits and behavior may be much more important. Many families with an income of $7,500 have a vastly better credit rating than some families living on $25,000 a year.

After getting the first answers on how much your income is, and how promptly you have paid your bills in the past, here are the important questions a good credit manager asks in order to make up his mind about taking your account. Remember, his selfish interest biases him in your favor. He is under pressure from the sales force to okay as many new charge accounts as possible.

Your employment record. If you work for a good firm, have a job that requires some education or some special skill, either intellectual or mechanical; that's favorable.

If you shift jobs frequently, do seasonal low-skilled labor, that's a red light to the credit man.

Income. Its stability is more important to the credit man than the amount. Credit men are leery of incomes based on commissions, tips, and one-shot deals, unless the applicant shows a steady total from these items over several years.

Marital status. Married men are generally considered

better credit risks than single men simply because young single men may not yet have a serious outlook on life. Unmarried women, however, usually are considered excellent risks.

If the applicant is married, a good credit man notes the number of children. If there are too many for the family income to provide for properly in his opinion, that's another red light.

Any sign that husband and wife battle, or that the children are neglected, is a very bright red light. Credit bureaus clip out such items from the papers and file them away.

Where you live can affect your credit standing decidedly. If you own a home or rent in a good neighborhood, that's favorable. If you live in furnished rooms, that may call for explanation. If you live in a questionable neighborhood, that's another red light.

Of course the credit bureau checks to see if you have judgments against you outstanding, or if you have been sued or garnished in the past or ever have bankrupted. These things in themselves will not keep you from getting credit. The credit man knows that, as often as not, misfortune rather than bad character is responsible for a past record of heavy debt. But if you have no current bank account, and have accumulated almost no tangible assets in life, that does raise a question.

Finally, and this is extremely important: The fact that a person applies for credit from a bank close to where he works or lives, or from a big store that he knows makes careful credit investigations, is one point in his favor. It's also in his favor if he doesn't seem to be in a huge hurry to get the cash or merchandise he is asking for.

The typical "dead beat" is more likely to approach a bank or loan company far from his home or employment, or to try a smallish store that he feels may not have top notch credit investigating facilities—and he (or she) nearly always is in a big hurry.

Of course, the bigger the amount you are trying to borrow the more searching the investigation. A bank or loan company will spend more of an investigator's time, which has to be paid for, in deciding on a $3,000 loan than it would for a $300 loan. For the bigger loan, the bank may ask that your wife sign the note with you if she works, or that you put up some savings bonds or stocks as collateral, or get a co-maker to sign.

After your credit is established, the way to keep it is to pay promptly. When expenses threaten to get out of hand, go to the bank and borrow enough additional money to meet the most pressing bills and avert bad credit reports. *Then economize promptly* until you get the new loan whittled down to size. The bank's personal loan department wants you to keep on borrowing from time to time—that's how it makes its living.

A very large number of Americans who live on salary are carrying too much debt. The rising number of personal or "grasshopper" bankruptcies proves that clearly. The rate of personal bankruptcies filed in Federal Courts went up from 48 per 100,000 in 1956 to 107 per 100,000 in 1962.

However, the total consumer debt, as a proportion of consumer income after taxes, went up in the same years only from 14.4 per cent to 15.3 per cent. Therefore, this problem of too much debt is a family problem rather than a public problem, *so far.*

Personally, I doubt if many working people, unless they have been more lucky than most, can meet this test of whether or not they are carrying too much debt. It is a consensus test devised by a number of credit men:

1. Do you keep less than $200 in cash or easily sold savings bonds on hand to meet an emergency?

2. Do your monthly installment payments (except for your home *mortgage*) exceed 20 per cent of your monthly income after taxes?

3. If you didn't make any new installment purchases, would it take more than one year to pay off all your present installment debts by speeding up payments on some of the longer term loans such as your car?

A "yes" answer to one of these doesn't mean too much; but, if the answer to all three is "yes," yours is one of the large number of American families which is carrying more debt than it should.

So, BEAR IN MIND . . .

Credit is a carefully protected business. Always be direct and honest when you apply.

More than 2,000 retail credit bureaus check the records of applicants for credit, as do many single-industry bureaus. And, they exchange information.

Your business credit rating is essentially a matter of how much money your firm has, and whether it pays bills promptly.

A large loan may require a co-maker. The position of co-maker can be risky, but this is a common practice. Careful!

Too much debt, in proportion to family income and family needs, is a common ailment among American families. Are you carrying too much debt? Quiz yourself (page 58).

9.   Where to Borrow Money

Thousands of people who have to borrow money pay through the nose, because *they don't know the best place to borrow.*

Generally speaking, a bank is the cheapest, fastest, and best place to borrow. Of course, not everybody is eligible to borrow from a bank. You must have something to pledge as collateral, or a steady job and pretty good credit rating; or you must have a friend who does qualify sign with you as co-maker. That makes *him* liable for the loan, if *you* don't pay.

Tragically, a great many people who are eligible for bank loans assume they are not. They think of bank loans as only for businessmen or rather high-salaried workers. That isn't the case at all. Small, unsecured personal loans are a comparatively new business for banks. They began in New York City about fifty years ago, but relatively few banks were in this business until after World War II. Now, nearly all larger banks make such loans. Very small banks do not make them, as a rule, because it takes a considerable volume of this business to make it pay; when a bank gets enough of it, it's extremely profitable.

If your job isn't steady enough to entitle you to bank credit, you will do well to try to join a *credit union* through the company you work for, or perhaps through your labor union. Credit union loan terms are not as cheap as bank terms, but are usually cheaper than those of small loan companiess.

The cheapest type of loan is one to be paid back all

in one sum. That way, you get the full use of the face amount of the loan, and you pay for it only by the simple interest of discount rate. As a rule, you must put up collateral (a bond or a stock certificate), or get a substantial co-maker to sign, or you must have exceptional credit standing, to get a personal loan on this basis. Otherwise, the bank is likely to insist on a loan to be paid back in installments. The bank has two excellent reasons for taking this attitude: it can be much surer of getting its money back on an unsecured loan in monthly installments and, as we shall see, the bank *makes about twice as much profit on installment loans* as on loans to be repaid in a lump sum.

When you borrow from the personal loan department of a bank, your estate will not have to repay the loan if you die before it's paid out. That's because the bank takes out short-term *insurance on your life for the amount of the loan*. This adds one-half of 1 per cent to your interest or discount cost, and it's a great bargain. Some personal finance companies, and many companies that finance sales of automobiles and appliances, also buy credit life insurance *in this manner;* in fact, it is increasingly becoming the case that if you die a month or so after buying a new car, the car is automatically paid for by the insurance company. But you can't assume this to be true; *you must make sure it is in the contract.*

Banks nearly always *discount* loans—instead of charging interest. What is the difference? Technically, interest is paid only after it is earned. That is, if you borrow $100 at 5 per cent for a year, the bank gives you the whole hundred dollars and at the end of the year you pay back $105. But usually the banks insist on a discount rate instead; you sign a note for $100 at a 5 per cent discount. The bank gives you $95 and you pay back $100 a year later. Here again, the bank is making a little more money on your loan than it would at simple interest. For you have the use of only $95 for a year instead of $100, yet you still pay $5 for the credit. The way it works out, the 5 per cent discount rate is equivalent to a simple interest rate of 5.26 per cent on the $95 you actually get. On small loans to be paid in a lump sum, the difference between a discount rate and a simple interest rate isn't very important; on a monthly installment loan of $1,000 or more, it can run into a considerable amount.

In the first place, the true interest rate of any installment loan is almost twice the stated annual rate because, averaged over the whole period of the loan, you only get the full use of about half the money. The rest you have repaid. And, when an installment loan is discounted for the full amount of the loan in advance, this increases the penalty.

As we said, banks virtually always insist on discounting loans. Finance companies writing automobile and appliance loans or financing installment accounts for stores may discount them, or they may charge interest as it becomes due. The difference can be considerable: $75 to $100 in the financing price of a car costing something under $3,000.

So, when the bank advertisement says that its current personal loan rate is 4½ per cent, that doesn't mean you pay only $4.50 *per annum* for each $100 borrowed. You pay, as we have seen, an extra ½ of 1 per cent for life insurance. Discounting adds from ¼ to ¾ of 1 per cent more to the gross annual rate. In addition, there are certain fees for processing which the bank is allowed, by the personal loan laws of each state, to add to the discount charge. If the loan is for more than one year, the basic charge per annum is multiplied by one and a half, two, or three as the case may be.

But no matter how long the loan runs, *if you are to pay it in monthly installments,* the *true* annual interest rate is about double the *stated* rate because you are paying interest or discount on money you no longer have the use of.

But, compared to the charges of the *small loan companies,* the installment personal loan from the bank is a great bargain. At most, the true cost of the bank installment loan can run up to 9 per cent a year; usually it's a bit less. In some states, the price of an installment loan from a small loan company can run up to around 40 per cent! Thus in Kansas, small loan companies are allowed to charge 3 per cent a month on a loan up to $300, or a straight dollar charge of $20.48 per annum per $100. Thus a one-year monthly installment loan for $300 would cost $61.44. But, for the whole year you have the use of only $150 of that $300. That's 40.9 per cent per annum! To be fair to Kansas, the companies have to cut the rate almost in half for larger loans. That is true in most states.

There are more than 2,000 of these small loan or consumer finance companies. They do an enormous business in about 13,000 offices. You only have to run down the table of rates they are allowed to charge to see that their profits are handsome, even on top of substantial overhead. Millions of people keep on borrowing from these companies *when they actually are eligible for bank loans* at a quarter to one-third of the rates they charge.

Why?

Sheer ignorance is the main cause. The chap who has never had a bank loan is afraid to go ask for one. Habit is another reason.

The small loan companies' big business, however, is lending to people who probably couldn't get bank loans: they have too many debts, they have court judgments against them, they have filed a petition in bankruptcy in recent years, they have a poor employment record or have been in trouble with the law. For its larger profit, the personal loan company is willing to take a chance on some of these people. However, don't get the idea that a good small loan company will lend to everybody who comes in the door. They all make investigations and they follow rules.

They lend a lot in small amounts for very short terms. And the stated interest is the exact interest they charge, high though it may be. If they charge 3 per cent a month, that 3 per cent is figured only on the declining balance.

There are other good places to borrow money besides banks, credit unions and small loan companies. Most people have life insurance policies and *you can borrow from the insurance company* up to most of the legal reserve of the policy simply by making application to the company through your agent. The charge, usually 5 to 6 per cent per annum simple interest, is paid with the subsequent premium installments. Veterans can borrow against the permanent G.I. insurance at 4 per cent simple interest. Many people who borrow on their life insurance never repay the loan, letting the company deduct it from the settlement after death.

Many fraternal societies have loan funds. There are specialized loan agencies that lend money for specific purposes for college tuition or other purposes. The rates of these special agencies usually are cheap because they often are non-profit, set up by organizations interested in certain social need. However, of late years, banks and finance companies have discovered good profits are to be made in reasonably priced college and prep school tuition loans, and have set up subsidiaries for this business.

So, when you need to borrow money, don't get panic stricken and rush into the first loan office you hear about and fill out an application. Think the matter over; think about who is likely to give you the best terms on a loan for the particular purpose you need. Spending money on interest is one of the hardest ways to spend money correctly.

It is an excellent idea for a young man or a couple to

make a small loan at a good bank as soon as they feel they are eligible for bank credit. Repay the loan promptly. Once you have established your credit at a bank it is much easier to borrow again if you suddenly need money. Then, you often can get the money within a couple of hours and it is even possible to arrange the matter largely by telephone.

Two strong words of caution:

Never withhold anything about your debts or your affairs from a bank you are asking for a loan, and never make a false statement of any kind. It can ruin your credit.

Watch out for "late charges." Bank loans, particularly installment loans, have very short grace periods or none at all. The same is true at small loan companies. If you make a habit of being a day or so late with the payments, the bank (or the loan company) won't complain. But it will sock you with hefty *"late charges"* that are added to your balance.

Loans on valuable jewelry, furs, collections of valuable stamps or art objects can be arranged through such institutions as the Provident Loan Society. Often, a chattel mortgage loan on such security can be obtained through investment bankers or mortgage brokers. Leading jewelers can give advice about such credit, as a rule.

Warnings about outright *loan sharks,* the hoodlums who lend $50 at $5 a week interest (520 per cent a year) and collect it with brass knucks if need be, hardly seem necessary after all the television, movie, newspaper and magazine exposure of their activities. But these characters still flourish in our larger cities, preying on weak, irresponsible people, particularly those addicted to gambling, narcotics or alcohol.

Every very large city has its *legitimate private money lenders,* people with money to lend in large amounts. These lenders deal mainly in business loans; they will lend to a big corporation for as little as 3 per cent a year.

But they will also take on a risky loan, charging from 10 to as high as 24 per cent a year, and a few of them will lend five million dollars without batting an eye.

Some of their loans are for personal purposes, too. About twenty years back, a prominent society girl of a family that was broke borrowed $50,000 from one of these lenders to finance a determined campaign to become a film star. She succeeded, paid off the loan, and became rich.

Then there was the well-known politician who went broke because he was too fond of poker and the ponies. A money lender advanced him $25,000 to finance the successful wooing of a very rich widow.

One of the most famous private money lenders was the late Sammy Bronstein of St. Louis. Sammy dealt in $10 to $50 advances to newspapermen, vaudeville actors, *filles de joie,* and similar chancy characters. One night Sammy got a frantic call from a regular client to come to a shady hotel. The guy was holding four jacks and needed $50 to stick for the showdown with almost $1,800 in the pot.

Sammy hurried over to the hotel, sized up the situation and made the loan. As the grateful client raked in the pot, Sammy firmly refused a proffered bonus, insisting he could not ethically accept more than his regular $5 fee—520 per cent per annum—"on such a small loan."

SO, BEAR IN MIND . . .

When you borrow, your bank is the best place to go.

You may not realize you *are* eligible for a bank loan.

One-lump-sum repayment is the cheapest way to borrow money. A lender earns twice as much from you if you repay in installments.

It's to your benefit, and it's your responsibility, to see that short-term life insurance for you is part of the loan contract.

The true interest rate you pay is higher than the stated

rate because you do not get to use all of the money all of the time.

Small loan companies are an expensive way to borrow. Many people pay these high fees when, in fact, they are eligible for loans at banks and credit unions—but they don't know this.

You can borrow on some insurance policies—at a low rate of interest.

Watch out for the loan sharks, both criminal and near-criminal. But, understand that there are legitimate private money lenders, too.

10. Watch Those Charge Accounts!

You can get stung a lot easier and a lot worse by credit charges for merchandise, particularly big ticket items like automobiles, than by borrowing cash.

Charge accounts always did cost, even back in the days when there was very little cash money in the rural parts of the United States and most people lived on credit and paid their bills monthly. No special credit charge was entered on his books by the merchant of that day, but he had to figure the credit risks and the length of time it took him to collect his money in calculating the markups on his merchandise.

In many stores of that era, price tags unashamedly said: "Cash $2.50, credit $3.25."

Nowadays the dealer gets his money at once on nearly everything he sells on credit, from banks or commercial finance companies. Only big department stores and high-grade specialty shops still use old-fashioned open account credit, and this is a small part of the department stores' business.

Selling merchandise of all kinds on credit has expanded enormously in the past twenty years. It has grown so much that there are types of stores, both in conventional retail shopping and the mail order business, that look to credit finance charges for their entire profit! Their merchandise markups cover only overhead and advertising costs. Anything they sell for cash does not contribute to the company earnings at all, only to volume.

Nor are the credit finance charges of all such companies extremely high. Their credit costs are not cheap, but they are not exorbitant because the companies depend on *volume* of credit rather than high rates for profit.

Merchandise credit rates, on installment sales or revolving accounts, normally are higher than the rates for personal loans at the bank—but not usually as high as those of the small loan companies. You generally save money by borrowing from the bank to buy instead of letting the store finance your installment purchases.

In some bigger installment sales, charges can be excessive if you buy from fly-by-night dealers. The used-car business in large centers, or in any area where there is a big market for cars among semi-literate or irresponsible people, is a happy hunting ground for shameless credit racketeers. More later, on that.

One of the most expensive types of credit, yet one of the most useful, is *the credit card.* Pioneered by the oil companies to enable the motorist to buy gasoline or get service without having to carry large amounts of cash, the credit card business has mushroomed into a giant since World War II. The credit card is a great convenience, a great protection against emergencies and robbery losses, and provides automatic records for tax purposes and business auditing—but it is expensive. The theory that the expense is borne mainly by the restaurants and other businesses the credit card companies sign up is only partly true. Whether they were eager to get credit card business, or forced by competition to accept it, many restaurants and hotels have had to raise their prices to cover credit card charges.

There can be no doubt, also, that the *possession of credit cards encourages personal extravagance.* This proved so true that credit companies have had to purge their card holder lists drastically to cut losses caused by personal extravagance or outright fraud.

A lost or stolen credit card can be a real hazard to the

original holder. He is legally responsible for anything charged on the lost card up to the hour he notifies the credit card company it is missing and for a certain period thereafter while the company is getting out warnings. Since the owner of the card may not discover its loss for some days, the thief can make a lot of hay. There are plenty of cases of charges running into thousands of dollars being made on a stolen credit card before its loss was discovered.

We said a moment ago that the old-fashioned open charge account now was limited to department stores and high-grade specialty shops. Perhaps we should qualify that; a considerable number of other stores do have open charge accounts on which you pay nothing for credit for the first thirty days. But, thereafter, a penalty charge goes on the account if you don't pay promptly.

The most popular retail credit plans currently used include—

The short-term plan of six to twelve months. Sometimes, all the credit charges are cancelled if payment is made in full within three months, but this is exceptional. The stores call these plans, which they operate themselves (although they may borrow cash against them), by various names such as Optional Charge Account, Budget Account, or Ten-Payment Plan. You sign a contract and agree to make payments on a regular scale. The true annual interest rate you pay on such accounts may run as high as 18 per cent, but often is less. It is not usually noted in the contract as an interest rate but as a fixed dollar charge which the stores' accountants arrive at by their own method.

The revolving credit plan is becoming the most popular retail type for all except big items. In its most common version, the revolving credit gives you most of the convenience of the old-fashioned open monthly charge account plus the advantage of paying installments that are only a fraction of the monthly balance. The store decides on the basis of your application what is the limit it is willing to carry your account for: $50, $100, or $500. You can buy that much at once and make monthly payments based on that amount. But you can't buy any more until you have *paid in* enough to reduce your balance so the new purchases will fall within the limit.

The revolving plan has changed a lot since it was first introduced in the mid-1930s. It has been combined with longer-term installment plans to make the limits more flexible and to add appliances and minor big-ticket items.

A totally new revolving plan called *the chart plan* has been adopted by many stores. The store does not attempt to limit your purchases rigidly; your monthly payments go up or down according to a fixed schedule based on your balance. Typically, the monthly payment for a $150 balance might be $11. But if you bought enough to raise your balance to $350, you would have to pay the store $65 that month. The next month your payment would go down again if you didn't buy more.

The cost for revolving plan credit is much in line with the shorter-term plans—not so cheap as bank credit but considerably cheaper than the fees of small loan companies. After all, the number of retailers who are out to make all their profits out of credit charges is not very big. Most merchants still want to make profits out of markups— they have to on cash sales—so they have an incentive not to let credit charges get too high.

Also merchants are increasingly worried lest the federal government crack down on them and regulate their credit charges, which they usually call "service charges" or "carrying charges." There was a big rumpus in Congress in 1962 over proposals that all retail plans carry detailed labels telling exactly how much was interest, how much for fees to cover investigation and collection, how much for credit life insurance, etc. Some states already have laws regulating retail credit charges. New York puts a ceiling of 1.5 per cent per month on unpaid balances up to $500 and 1 per cent above that. This works out to a true annual interest rate of approximately 18 per cent.

Professor James Allen Jung of the University of Chicago Business School made a comparative study of retail credit costs in a number of our leading cities. He found the department stores generally had the cheapest plans, and the so-called discount stores had the most expensive plans! Much of what the discount stores took off the "markup" they recaptured in the credit contract. However, to be fair, we must remember that discount houses sell mainly for cash.

The most important thing Professor Jung discovered, though, was that while bank credit costs are constant within a community and vary only by about 2 per cent in true annual interest cost across the country, the installment credit charges of finance companies and dealers on appliances vary tremendously within a given city. They also vary startlingly from city to city—as much as 50 per cent!

Here are some of the variations Professor Jung found from his survey of appliance sales financed by dealers themselves or through commercial finance companies, reported in *The Journal of Business*:

Boston	12.9%	to 20.4%
Chicago	14.8%	to 27.7%
Cleveland	14.8%	to 22.1%
Detroit	14.8%	to 22.2%
New York	14.8%	to 18.4%
Pittsburgh	13.8%	to 20.3%
St. Louis	14.8%	to 18.4%
San Francisco	9.2%	to 22.2%

Note that a variation of 9 percentage points can mean a swing of 50 percent in the actual cost.

The frequent recurrence of 14.8 per cent as the minimum true annual interest on appliance installment accounts suggests that's about the figure the canny consumer should aim at having to pay.

We'll have a separate chapter on the cost of financing the purchase of an automobile.

So, bear in mind . . .

Retail credit is useful, but you pay for it.

The cost of retail credit is higher than that for a bank loan, but it is less than the interest charged by a small loan company.

There are several credit plans, and their costs vary. Different stores have different plans. It is something to consider when you open an account.

Credit cards have their uses. Still, they are no exception to the rule that credit costs. In this case you—and everyone—must pay in the form of higher prices.

Discount stores, which may sell more cheaply, are based on cash sales. Often, their credit plans are more expensive than those of regular department stores.

11. Renting Versus Owning

When a young couple have saved their first two or three thousand dollars and have their first baby or two, the husband or wife or both inevitably get the itch to buy a house.

But in a few weeks they are overwhelmed by conflicting advice about what kind of house to buy, where to buy one, or whether it's wise to buy at all.

In plain truth, it's not the easiest thing in the world to decide when is the right time for a young couple to buy their own home. Nor can a general, completely honest answer be given to the question of whether it's cheaper to own or rent.

The federal income tax law vastly favors the home owner over the renter—by allowing the home owner to deduct mortgage interest and real estate taxes, while the renter cannot deduct that part of his rent which his landlord pays out in mortgage interest and realty taxes. But Congress could change that anytime.

In periods of deflation such as the depressed 1930's and many periods of somewhat stagnant stability, there's no doubt but it was cheaper to rent. All through the 1930's, houses and apartments were for rent in huge numbers across the country at figures way below the cost of buying and maintaining equivalent living space in a house or co-operative apartment of your own.

There is a considerable number of such apartments and houses for rent in many cities and villages today. They rent for figures that do not return a profit to the landlord, and the federal tax authorities regularly allow him to take a loss on their rental in his income return. Even brand-new luxury apartments and rental houses (if you can find such houses for rent) will show a loss for tax purposess when the depreciation is figured in.

Of course there's a big joker in this. Although both the income tax laws and sound accounting practice permit and call for depreciating a rental home or apartment building, yearly—often at 5 per cent—the market value may very well go up while the property is being depreciated on the books. The value may go up two to five times as fast as it is being written off in depreciation! In a good location, it wasn't at all uncommon for even old houses to double or triple in market value between 1946 and 1960.

There are other reasons why *it may be cheaper for many couples to keep on renting*. If the husband is in a business where he is likely to be moved around frequently, then, buying a home and selling it when a transfer comes along entails a lot of trouble and may mean considerable risk of loss.

If you live in New York City and for some reason cannot undertake to commute, you haven't any option in the matter. You have to rent—until you have made enough headway in the world to get out to the suburbs or until you have really climbed the totem pole and can afford a co-op apartment. Co-op apartments in New York run very high.

Most people own their homes because they want them, not because they hope to save money. That being true, they virtually always (I never heard of a contrary case) deliberately plan to spend a great deal more on their own house than they ever did on renting. *They are buying more*: more interior space, a yard, a garage, proximity to a better school, quiet, closeness to a beach, nice scenery, appearance of the house for personal satisfaction and status, the hope of an atmosphere in which they will make friends, and in which the children will have the incentive to do better in school and to make better marriages.

Even when you put in all these extra items, it is not possible to give a pat answer to the question of whether it's cheaper to rent or buy.

But I can make some honest and accurate observations about the matter.

The factory or office or shop worker who must work in one of our larger cities usually can rent better accommodations (for the proportion of his income that he should pay for housing) than he can get by buying. In the smaller villages and countryside, the small-salaried worker is more apt to be able to afford buying a house.

At the other end of the scale, the rich man, in a high tax bracket, simply cannot afford to rent a home. He needs the tax-deduction benefits that come with the mortgage on a big house or a deluxe co-op apartment.

For the rest of us, the answer to the question is somewhere in between—dependent on our individual situation.

But there's room for one or two more observations. Some people who switch from renting to owning expect a great many more financial benefits than they actually get. I was reminded of this forcibly a year or so back when a friend told me he was buying his first house and expected to be able to depreciate it for tax purposes!

Only income property can be depreciated for tax purposes. If you have a two-family house and rent out one apartment, you can depreciate the house and deduct half the depreciation from the rent you get on the apartment along with the other expenses of maintaining it such as heat, decorating, repairs and so forth.

Others rush into home buying fondly imagining the $150 a month they will pay the bank that holds the mortgage is going to be "like rent" in that it is going to cover almost everything.

It sure won't.

It may not even cover insurance, although that is not usually a back-breaking item, and most of the time the monthly payment to the bank does cover insurance.

But it doesn't cover heating and, as the family gets bigger and older, heating gets ever more expensive.

The heating bill for a three-bedroom house anywhere in the northern states can run above $30 monthly, and maybe considerably more in January and February. Lots of young couples don't realize that, and often their warm love nest becomes rather chilly. (Having been close to the oil heating industry as an insurance advisor to the New York Oil Heating Association for the past sixteen years, I have learned that oil heat is indeed the cheapest and safest method of heating your home.)

It doesn't cover mowing the lawn, trimming the hedges, spraying the bugs on the flowers, having the septic tank drained every two or three years, the water bills that pile up with an automatic washing machine and a family of six, or the installments on the larger quantity and better quality furniture you decided the very first home of your own deserved.

When you rented, you never thought of decorating as being terribly expensive. If you couldn't talk the landlord into repainting your apartment, you hired a chap to do it or did it yourself and the bill wasn't enormous.

The work wasn't too well done either; in fact, more often than not it was downright sloppy, a real jackleg job.

But your own house now, that's something else, brother! You and your wife are astonished at how quickly the family can scuff and spill and kick the joint apart— both inside and out. You soon find out that either you spend a certain number of hours every month around the calendar painting *and* spackling and caulking, or else you can count on a painting bill of a thousand bucks or so every three years. Doing it yourself, of course, is vastly cheaper—but it takes a lot of time. And after all, is a chap who isn't used to doing it really being smart when he gets up on a high ladder to do outside painting? He's risking his life and his family's livelihood to save as little as $200.

Repairs to windows, doors, plumbing, trees, cellar walls and the floors will cost more in time and money than you think.

Of course, if you like mowing the grass and spackling and painting and couldn't do anything more profitable with your time and money, buying a house when you are very young may be the most satisfying investment of your life.

But let's consider a hypothetical young man named Tom Jones who, in 1955, was selling life insurance for Marvelous Life of New York. Tom heard some of his bosses say that Marvelous Life stock was a sure-fire investment with huge gain possibilities. He had $2,600 in the bank and he wanted to put it in his company's stock. But his wife, Ethel, wanted him to put the $2,600 in the down payment on a $12,000 house. Tom yielded.

By May, 1963, by dint of much hard work and sacrifice, Tom and Ethel could figure the house had gone up in value to $17,500, but they still owed half the original purchase price.

And what had happened to Marvelous Life stock meanwhile? If Tom had put the $2,600 in his company's stock in 1955, and just left it there without any care or hard work or any further watering with dollar bills, his investment would have grown by May, 1963, to $143,000!

This is an extreme case. I cite it to show that, from a strictly financial point of view, *a home is seldom a real growth investment.* It grows in value in good time, but that entails hard work, and it can be a source of great loss in times of depressions.

When a young couple put their first savings into a home, they may be gambling away their whole lives on a relatively poor investment—and find themselves in the coming years without the small amount of capital needed to take advantage of real opportunities.

Cynics will argue that if Tom had been a real go-getter, he would have managed to borrow the $2,600 *and* buy the Marvelous Life stock in addition to buying the home to please his wife. But most of us are not real go-getters; most of us are like our imaginary Tom Jones and listen to the womenfolk who don't want to take risks and who have an emotional yearning for a house of their own, which often doesn't make good sense. And many a man, by yielding to his wife's insistence in this respect, *is buying a lifetime of poverty and frustration* for both of them. How often, do you suppose, our imaginary Tom Jones would throw it up to Ethel that she talked him out of the great opportunity of their lives?

Since 1961 it has been possible to rent automobiles so cheaply that *many people who do not use a car every day might be well advised to consider renting instead of owning.* Not only is it cheaper in many cases but it eliminates the worry of liability insurance cancellations and of parking a car overnight in the streets if you live in a big city where garaging is expensive.

There is now good reason to believe that in many cities the cheap rental agencies—$5 to $6 a day plus gasoline plus nine cents a mile—are here to stay. At that rate, you need to use a car quite a bit to make owning one pay.

Of course, for rural or suburban living, an owned automobile is a necessity and the chap who must drive fifteen miles or more to work every day must have his own jalopy.

The fellow who uses a car all day long for business may rent much more cheaply, in the long run. That's because the federal income tax rules are exactly opposite for business property to the tax rules governing property for personal use.

If you rent a car and use it only for business, the entire rental is a deductible business expense; whereas, if you own the car, the purchase price is a *capital outlay* and not deductible as ordinary *expense*. You can depreciate it for taxes, but only if you use it regularly for business.

In fact, the tax advantage of renting cars, trucks, machinery, buildings and equipment of all kinds—plus the tremendous advantage to business of not tying up too much money in the purchase prices of these things—has caused a large new activity called *the leasing industry* to spring up in the era since World War II to serve business and industry of all kinds. This is now a business running into billions of dollars a year.

Some folks may ask at once, why, if the tax advantages and capital advantages are so great, don't most businesses rent everything and not own anything?

The answer is that everything is relative. Some essential things can't be rented, they simply must be owned. And it sometimes is unsafe not to own a valuable machine or a highly strategic business location. How often do you see a sign on a store that is selling out with the laconic explanation, "Lost our lease." Somebody bought the building or obtained a term lease on it, right out from under the firm, forcing it out of business.

And the profits of owning a highly productive machine often are so great that tying up capital in it is well worthwhile, and the tax advantages of renting it become trifling.

So, bear in mind . . .

The right *time* to buy, in your life, is as important as any other consideration in selecting a home.

Federal income taxes favor the home owner.

A house offers more than money savings, it *gives* more.

Wealthy people should own a house for the tax advantages alone, if for no other strong reason.

Only income property can be depreciated for tax purposes.

The mortgage payment is but part of the monthly expense. Remember, there's heating, lawn care, repairs and all.

Do-it-yourself often is the wrong solution to house upkeep.

All things considered, a home is seldom a good growth investment.

Automobiles can often be rented as required at a good saving over owning one. And, there are tax advantages to renting a car if you use it for business.

As with owning a home, owning a car can sometimes be the better decision in your particular case. This applies, too, to business locations and equipment.

Your best bet for heating your home as to safety and cost has proved to be oil, based on my experience.

12. Buying a House

Having decided wisely or unwisely to buy a house, you next must decide how much you can afford to spend.

There used to be a cardinal rule of family budgeting that about one week's pay per month should be devoted to rent. Rent is shelter and the idea was that the one week's pay for each month's shelter should include the cost of heating.

But that cardinal rule gained acceptance in days long before the average family had to pay federal income tax at rates of 20 per cent and up, in days when real estate taxes were much lower and before an automobile became a necessity. It is a rare family today that can make both ends meet, if almost 25 per cent of the gross monthly income goes into shelter. Yet many families attempt it.

The amount you pay monthly on your mortgage, plus real estate taxes and insurance, plus heating is roughly equivalent to rent. And, under today's conditions, *this sum should be somewhat less than a week's income.* Therefore, the first consideration is to determine how much you can pay monthly for these items—and then hunt for houses whose carrying charges and heating costs will be within this figure.

If you have inherited some money or saved quite a bit and can make a very big down payment—40 or 50 per cent—you can carry a bigger house than most people, without burdening yourself. But buying too expensive a house on a small or even a normal down payment is to invite disaster.

You likely will find that if you are going to pay 20 to 25 per cent down, then *the total price of the kind of house you can afford to carry and heat will hardly exceed twice your annual income.* I am talking now about the incomes of ordinary mortals; let the rich solve their own problems—or pay someone to worry for them.

Now that you have figured out that much, you start reading the real estate ads, talking to friends and riding about the city and the countryside looking for a house. Ouch! That word "countryside" reminds me that I have just committed a monumental blooper; I have forgotten all about *commuting costs!*

If you are moving from a city apartment to a suburban home, you are going to have to get to and from work. Whether you drive or take a train or bus, it's going to cost quite a bit more than going to work on a city bus or subway.

If you drive, you have gasoline to pay for and perhaps parking charges and, in most states, the insurance companies raise your liability premiums if you drive to work daily. Also, *you might need a second car* for your wife to shop in and haul the kids around; distances are terrific in many modern suburban areas. If you are going to commute to work by train or bus, the cost may be $30 a month or more—and all these charges must be taken into consideration in reaching the all-important decision as to how much you can afford to spend each month on carrying and heating the house.

Optimism is mankind's most ambivalent characteristic; it gives us the drive and courage to move forward, but it also gets us into a heck of a lot of trouble; and it causes an awful lot of couples to under-estimate the expenses and buy more house than they really can afford.

On the other hand, buying a house that's much too small is equally unsatisfactory. It takes only two children for the family to outgrow a very small house and the lack of individual privacy in such cramped quarters can lead to husband and wife hurling insults and dishes at each other, whereas in a bigger house each could sulk in privacy until overcome by a yearning to kiss and make up.

The reasons that will cause you to decide on a particular house probably will not be economic and so are no great concern of this book. However, I would like to point out a few economic factors to remember—

If you buy a house in a neighborhood that is obviously running to seed because the house is in excellent condition and seems a bargain, you are making a bad investment. *Location is everything* in a real estate investment. An old house in only fair condition in an excellent neighborhood often can be repaired or even modernized at reasonable cost; a well-built house in a bad neighborhood depreciates as fast as the shanty next door.

Check on the sewerage situation. If sewers are not already in but are not far away you may get socked with a staggering *sewer assessment* in a few years. If there are no sewers for miles then you can assume the community is going to continue to depend on septic tanks. The upkeep on these is modest.

Low property taxes are not necessarily a bargain. Communities that are stingy about spending money for schools, police and fire protection, public welfare, and keeping the streets paved are often unpleasant and unsafe to live in, and real estate values may start going down any time.

In deciding between an old house and a new house, remember that while older houses often are roomier and more solidly built, they are not usually so conveniently arranged as a modern house and frequently are more expensive to heat. Yet, since they were built in times when labor and materials were cheaper, they often do have the restful charm of spaciousness.

A house with exterior walls of brick, stucco, asbestos cement, or prepainted aluminum siding (the paint is baked on) will not require outside painting except for the trim. This can be a big saving over the years compared with clapboard or cedar shingle walls.

Unless you have a decided talent for it, do not plan to be a "do-it-yourself" expert. The risk of falling from a ladder is just one of the problems.

I once had as an insurance client, a dentist with a practice that netted him fifty thousand a year. At his wife's insistence he bought an old run-down house that was charming to look at but needed extensive repairs. Tragically, the dentist decided to do them himself, and bought a set of power tools.

Coming home one night after quite a long day with his drills and forceps, he went into his workshop and started cutting some lumber for new wall panelling.

In two minutes, he had cut his arm so badly it had to be amputated.

The charming but impractical old house was not just a fifty thousand loss—it had destroyed a fifty thousand dollar a year livelihood.

Another pitfall in buying an old house and repairing it is the *mechanic's lien*. Most people don't know that when you hire a contractor or a mechanic to buy materials and do a job on your house you become liable, in many states, for any materials he may buy on credit for the job.

I know of a chap who paid a painter a bill running to $2,000 on an extensive job on a very large house—then was sued for $400 by a paint store because the painter had not paid his bill! The painter had vanished.

The home owner learned sadly from his lawyer that, even though he had not personally ordered the paint and had paid the painter, the paint store had a mechanic's lien on his house. He had to pay it off in order to protect his title.

So, BEAR IN MIND . . .

The monthly costs of your house, all together, should be less than one week's income.

When you can give 20 to 25 per cent as a down payment, the total cost of the house should equal one year's income.

Don't forget the expense of commuting to work, if you move out of town.

Too little and too much house are equally bad. Choose carefully.

Location is as important as any single factor when selecting a home. Among other things, check for future sewer assessments.

Low property taxes may be a bad bargain—it may indicate poor community services.

The outside finish of the house determines whether an expensive regular painting will be required.

When you hire repairmen, be careful. A Mechanic's Lien can be placed against you for materials used to repair your home—even though you paid the workman for them.

13. How to Get a Mortgage

The commonest mistake people make in buying a house is to buy it too soon—before they have saved enough for an adequate down payment.

The Veterans Administration mortgage which enables the ex-G.I. to buy a home on twenty or twenty-five year term with no down payment is frankly a reward for military service; *it is not a good business deal* for anyone except the lending institution that collects the interest.

It may be a good personal arrangement for the ex-soldier, but he shouldn't kid himself that he is a real homeowner during the early life of the mortgage. He is building up equity in the house much too slowly. This is proven by the fact that, when banks or other lending institutions have to foreclose these VA mortgages, the houses nearly always are advertised for re-sale with no down payment. The original holder hasn't accumulated any equity to sell.

While some houses can be bought for down payments as low as 10 per cent—even less when the market is slow —*it's much better to pay 20 or 25 per cent down* if you can. That way, you start out with enough equity in the house to give you both a big incentive to keep the place up and something to realize on in case you have to sell because of a job transfer or some similar reason.

Mortgage credit is much easier to get in some years than in others, depending on business conditions. In the summer of 1963, for example, mortgage money was plentiful with some lending institutions having trouble getting enough loans to put their money to work. This condition has been caused by the entry of the big city commercial banks into the mortgage business, which they had stayed out of for many years.

Only about four years ago, home mortgage money was short. To get a good level-payment mortgage on some houses it was necessary then to pay an "under the table" bonus to the lending institution. And many sellers of houses had to "take back" second mortgages on a part of the purchase price to clinch the deal.

The real estate agent who sells you your house usually will get you a mortgage if you wish him to. Up to the point where he takes your deposit, the real estate agent represents the seller who pays him his commission, but from that moment on, a good real estate agent is as eager to help you as to serve his client. Frequently, he will get you as good or better mortgage as you possibly could get for yourself. But it won't do any harm to look yourself if you wish.

If you are in a great hurry, you may have to engage the services of a *professional mortgage broker*. He will charge you a fee of $50 or more and he is not likely to get you a better mortgage than you or your real estate agent can get, but he may get it much more quickly.

Mortgage loans are made by:

> Federal savings and loan associations
> Building and loan associations
> Insurance companies
> Savings banks
> Mortgage companies
> Private lenders
> Commercial banks.

The Federal savings and loan associations perhaps have the biggest volume of home mortgage business at present.

They advertise vigorously and there is at least one in almost every community in the country.

There are many varieties of mortgages, but they boil down to three or four:

The Conventional Mortgage. This is the old-fashioned mortgage of which so many were foreclosed in the early years of the Great Depression. You pay the interest and perhaps a small payment on the principal quarterly or semi-annually. The mortgage runs for perhaps ten years and *most of the principal is unpaid when it expires;* then it must be renewed or liquidated by a new mortgage from another lender. The interest rate usually is 6 per cent, and it is a "true" interest rate since you have the full use of virtually the whole sum during the life of the mortgage. You look after your own tax and insurance payments.

The conventional mortgage rarely is written on homes nowadays, but it is used for commercial property and apartment buildings.

The Level Payment Mortgage. This is the type now used almost universally for homes. You pay the bank or savings and loan association a fixed monthly sum to cover interest, payments on principal, taxes, and, sometimes, insurance. The part of the monthly payment covering interest and principal cannot be changed, but the bank can raise your monthly tax trust fund payment when taxes go up. At the beginning, the greater part of the fixed payment goes to interest, but there is an immediate reduction of principal. The interest payment goes down month by month, and the principal payment goes up.

There are many level payment plans; they range roughly from thirteen-and-a-half years to more than twenty years. *The VA mortgage,* already mentioned, is a level-payment mortgage.

The FHA Mortgage is simply a level-payment mortgage insured as to the lender (not the borrower) under the Federal Housing Act. In order to be so insured it must conform with rather strict federal regulations, and the amount of interest and fees that can be charged openly is strictly regulated. Also, if a house is eligible for an FHA mortgage, it has *passed inspection* on certain important fundamentals and thus has to be in fair condition.

However, there are many non-FHA mortgages that are about as good as the FHA-insured loan.

The Life Insured Mortgage is a package consisting of a level-payment mortgage and an ordinary life or term insurance policy. It was invented by insurance companies to compete with the Federal savings and loan associations for mortgage business. If you have such a mortgage and you die, even the very day you borrow the money, your widow automatically gets the home free and clear. Of course, the life insured mortgage costs more—you have to pay for the insurance—but some insurance companies offer them at very attractive rates.

The Second Mortgage is something put on a house to cover a gap between the amount of cash you have for a down payment and the amount you can get in first mortgage money when the mortgage market is bad. It also may represent a loan you have put on a house in which you have considerable equity to raise money for an emergency. Second mortgages seldom run for more than five years and often for only two. If your equity in the house is very large, you may be able to get a second mortgage at reasonable interest, but if it's risky—and remember the lender can't collect a penny on it until tax claims, mechanic's liens, and the first mortgage are satisfied—the interest may be high, 7 to 10 per cent. Second mortgages other than "take-backs" are written mainly by special brokers.

However, many second mortgages are take-backs. The seller simply agrees to take part of his down payment in the form of a second mortgage, either on a monthly level payment basis for two to five years or a lump sum deferred payment after one or two years. The interest on the take-back second mortgage usually is 5 per cent; occasionally the seller is so anxious to complete the deal he charges no interest at all on the second mortgage.

You may see the term *"Savings Bank mortgage"* in real estate ads. That means a mortgage written by a savings bank; it probably is a typical level-payment plan if written on a one-family home, a conventional mortgage if on an apartment house.

One other type of home mortgage is becoming increasingly important. It is the *shorter term level-payment mortgage* on pre-fabricated or shell homes. These are written by the pre-fab manufacturers or the finance companies they work with. They usually run seven or eight years and the interest charges are higher than for FHA mortgages but are not excessive.

Typically, these mortgages finance the full erected price of a pre-fabricated or shell home ranging from $2,000 to $5,000 (sometimes more). The customer must have paid cash for a lot with access to a road and electricity and having a water supply and cesspool. He pledges this lot in lieu of a down payment on the house.

These pre-fab and shell houses have been sold by the thousands in recent years to working people and retired people in the South, Midwest, and far West. Most of the buyers could not meet the credit requirements for an FHA mortgage. During the 1950s, some of the manufacturers and their finance companies were much too lenient in their credit on these homes and had to repossess thousands of them. They have since tightened their requirements substantially.

When you apply for a mortgage, the house itself is the principal security. The lending institution will lend only a certain percentage of the value it puts on the property in its own appraisal. However, the institution investigates your personal record and credit standing, just as a bank does when you apply for a personal loan and may turn you down, even though the house itself is excellent security, if your personal credit is really bad.

Once issued, the mortgage is a negotiable security and rarely allows the lender to block the sale of the property to anyone else. *If the new purchaser defaults* on the mortgage, *the lender can come back to you to collect.* Therefore, in selling a house, it is nearly always advisable to make the buyer get a new mortgage of his own and use part of the proceeds to pay off the balance of your mortgage. Otherwise, the lending institution must be induced to investigate the credit of the new buyer, accept him in your place and give you a written release. This rarely is done, but it might happen if the bank regarded the existing mortgage as a desirable loan and the new buyer as a good risk.

So, BEAR IN MIND . . .

The G.I. loan for home buyers is really not a good deal. If you can, it's better to pay 20 to 25 per cent down.

Check the several sources of home mortgages, and compare rates.

You may benefit by the advice of a professional mortgage broker in choosing from the several different forms of home mortgage.

A mortgage is a negotiable security. If you sell your home and the new owner defaults on the mortgage, *you* can be held responsible for the payments.

14. Swing Low, Sweet Chariot

Next to the house and often long before it, the biggest expenditure of the average family is for an automobile.

I have already pointed out that, for some big city dwellers, it is cheaper and more convenient to rent a car than to own one.

But suppose you don't live in a big city, or you are one of those urban residents who really needs to own a car, then you have a number of decisions to make, decisions that can mean several thousand dollars to you during the most important years of your life.

Just as many families undoubtedly buy too much house, too soon, many families and many single folk buy *too much automobile and too soon.* The difference is in the gasoline consumption, tire replacement cost and other upkeep. These costs are substantially lower for a small European car or an American compact than for a big car. The little European cars get well over thirty miles to the gallon of fuel. Insurance rates sometimes are cheaper on the small cars. They are far easier to park and, of course, they cost less—except for the expensive sports cars.

On the other hand, the small car is tiresome for long trips and the *cheap* small car may have a relatively short life. And, for *some* of the European small cars, it is not easy to get service in the United States outside of the metropolitan centers—and then it may take days compared with hours to get an American car serviced.

If you live in the suburbs or a smallish city and have several children, unquestionably you need a good-sized car, very possibly a station wagon. Even so, many people probably buy a big nine-passenger wagon with a big engine when a seven-passenger car with a smaller engine is really more suited to their needs and purse.

Don't buy too big a car just because it looks big, sleek and powerful! It is a little like burning up dollar bills.

Next decision is *whether to buy a new or a used car*. Detroit propaganda to the contrary, the used car, particularly the cheap jalopy, costs less over the years as a straight financial proposition—considerably less. But there are many other things to be considered.

If you buy a new car there is the question of whether you should plan to trade it in every three years, or to maintain it extra well and keep it for its full life—which can be ten or even fifteen years. Here again, the auto industry's propaganda is wrong. On a straight dollars-and-cents basis *it is much cheaper to drive the car for many years than to trade it in frequently*.

But you may not have the alternative. If your business compels you to drive 20,000 miles a year or more, taking long trips, you will have to trade the car in at regular intervals because it is getting more than normal wear and the life of an automobile that gets hard usage has to be measured in miles, not years.

Similarly, people in many professions definitely need to drive comparatively new cars. A physician needs a relatively new car not only for the sake of complete reliability and personal comfort but for the same reason that he needs an attractive office; it's human nature for patients to raise their eyebrows and begin to wonder if the doctor's chariot looks shabby. Many salesmen and people in other businesses also feel, with sound economic justification, that they cannot afford to be seen driving around in an eight-year-old car.

But others trade in their cars frequently for no sound economic reason—just to pamper an emotional urge to have something new and shiny. That will cost you a lot. Let's see how much it will cost you.

Suppose you pay $3,000 for a new car and the finance charge for three years on a low down payment is about $500. You trade it in at the end of three years and you trade in again at the end of six years. Each time you get a $1,200 allowance on the old car and the finance charge on the new car is lower than the original $500. At the end of nine years it will have worked out something like this:

First car	$3,500
Second car	2,150
Third car	2,150
	$7,800
Less trade-in value of third car......	1,200
Basic cost for nine years	$6,600

Now suppose you keep the same car nine years, spending a little extra to maintain it and drive it an average of only a little over 10,000 miles a year. That works out this way:

Cost of car	$3,500
Extra maintenance of $100 after first year	800
	$4,300
Nominal value of nine-year-old car	100
Basic cost for nine years	$4,200

You are $2,400 ahead of the chap whose situation compels him to trade in his car every three years and, since your nine-year-old car still may be good for three to six years, you may gain $500 to $1,000 more by keeping it up and driving it.

Now, let's consider the jalopy. Suppose you buy five jalopies at an average of $600 over nine or ten years, trading them in at $100 allowance as soon as they start to cost you too much money. That will work out this way:

Five jalopies at $600 with financing. . . .	$3,500
Less trade-in allowances on four cars. . . .	400
	$3,100
Estimated extra maintenance at $50 a year	450
	$3,550
Trade-in value of fifth car	100
Basic cost for nine or ten years.	$3,450

You are $3,150 ahead of the chap who buys new cars and trades them in. But, before we let parsimony run away with us, let's remember what I said in the first chapter about the folly of failing to spend enough money when it is wise and desirable. For one thing, the chronic jalopy driver has to have some head for mechanics; he must be able at least to suspect what is wrong with his old car when it has the miseries, else he will be robbed on maintenance or be out of a car frequently. And on a long trip, a jalopy can develop some very expensive miseries—with no warranty protection.

So, in spite of the big apparent saving, the jalopy habit has its financial hazards too.

One inducement to keep jalopies instead of relatively new cars is the high incidence of cars being hit and suffering body damage while parked—and you can't find the villain to collect. It isn't nearly so painful to have the fender of a $400 jalopy stove in this manner as to come out some morning and find a fender and a door smashed in on your nearly new Buick by some unidentified drunk.

In advising against buying too much car, I intend no disparagment of the big car for those who need it and can afford it. The American fine car is dollar-for-dollar about the finest merchandise buy in the world. It is remarkably economical to operate in proportion to its weight, is long-lived if you want to run it for years, and its comfort and safety and beauty provide tremendous personal satisfaction. *But, an automobile must serve you;* you must not work to support the car—and that's what you will be doing if you buy a fine, big car before you can afford it.

Financing the purchase of an automobile is trickier than borrowing cash or financing merchandise at most stores. The same Professor Jung of the University of Chicago who found the remarkable variances in the cost of financing purchases of appliances in various cities found just as great divergencies in financing the purchase of new cars and better used cars. Here are some of the variations Professor Jung found. The figures are true annual interest rates rather than the stated rates:

	DEALER FINANCING	BANK FINANCING
Boston	9.7% - 15.8%	9 %
Chicago	11.1% - 13.6%	10.6%
Cleveland	9.7% - 15.4%	10.8%
Denver	9.7% - 15 %	9.7%
Detroit	11.7% - 13.6%	11.6%
New York	11.5% - 14 %	9.7%
St. Louis	8.8% - 15.8%	9.5%
Pittsburgh	11.7% - 13.6%	9.6%
San Francisco	11.7% - 14.4%	11.4%

The first thing we notice is that a considerable number of dealers finance at bank rates, probably through arrangements with local banks. Next we notice that 9.7 per cent is the frequent true annual interest rate—equal to a stated rate of about 4¾ per cent, which probably also includes credit life insurance in many cases.

The difference between a true annual interest rate of 9.7 per cent and something like the maximum 15.8 per cent in Boston is about $60 per thousand of the face amount of the loan—$180 on a $3,000 balance.

Unfortunately, these variations only scratch the surface of the financial pitfalls in buying a car. There are not so many of these in the new car business. New car purchases are nearly always financed by banks or by the large reputable finance companies having agreements with the automobile manufacturers and dealer groups.

But in the used, and in the so-called "nearly new," car businesses, *rackets abound.* One of the commonest is the *"hidden load."* You buy a used car costing $1,000 or more. The dealer quotes you a financing package including collision insurance which he tells you is quite expensive but is required by the finance company. You swallow this statement and sign the contract. The dealer sells your contract to a small finance company, which in turn sells it to a bank. Then the insurance company sends you a carbon memorandum of the actual cost of the insurance and you discover it was only about half as much as the dealer indicated. Indignantly, you get out your copy of the contract and discover the dealer has ingeniously left the space for the cost of the insurance blank and has lumped interest, insurance and other fees in a single item called financing charges. Nowhere does the contract contain the figure for interest which the dealer quoted you. What has happened is that he and the small finance company have loaded the finance charge with an extra $100 or so and have falsely told you it was for insurance.

But your contract doesn't show it, so you're stuck. If you complain to the bank that has bought your contract, the chances are the bank won't even answer your letter

unless you are a depositor. The bank is an innocent holder
in due course and doesn't care, even though its officers
could tell from personal experience what has happened by
looking at your contract. Chances are the bank not only
will ignore your letter but will keep right on buying notes
from the same small finance company—knowing it is in
the habit of defrauding customers. It's profitable business.
Some bankers, particularly in small banks, aren't too
scrupulous about principle—if they aren't legally involved.

Even some of the bigger finance companies are not
above making you take out a *three-year-collision policy*
at once on a new car. The premium for the whole three
years is added to the carrying charges. You are thus paying
a substantial interest charge, in effect, on your insurance
for the second and third years. If you buy your insurance
separately from your insurance broker, you only have to
buy for one year at a time, and you save money.

There are worse rackets in used and "almost new"
car financing. A few years back, the *New York World-
Telegram & Sun* exposed a particularly vicious one. New
York law (and the laws of most states) is pretty strict on
the maximum interest rates that may be charged an individual—but in lending to a corporation the sky's the
limit. Some sharpie used car dealers conceived the idea
of setting up a dummy corporation with the purchaser of
a car owning all the stock. Then the customer, who invariably was a dummy in more ways than one, was charged
true annual interest rates up to and exceeding 40 per cent!
The New York authorities broke up that racket.

In 1963, the New York *Journal-American* reported the
revival of an older and equally vicious used car financing
racket. You buy a car from a dealer and it is financed
through a small loan company. You pay regularly on it
for months but aren't too careful to pay the very day the
installment is due; after all, most banks and finance com-

panies don't particularly care if you're a few days late—
they just charge you extra interest and a penalty charge.

But this particular company has a sharp scheme. It
waits patiently until you have paid out more than half
the loan. Then suddenly, without warning, it sends a
man to repossess your car just a few days after a payment
is due. Perhaps the car is picked up from where you left
it parked and you report it missing to the police. But next
morning comes a letter from the finance company. Your
car has been repossessed for non-payment of an installment
and is going to be auctioned off the next day. You can
pay off the remaining balance of the loan at once or bid
on it at the auction to protect your equity if you wish.
You scurry around, raise some money and show up at the
auction—only to be told that your car already has been
sold, that it didn't even bring the balance due and you
owe a deficiency on the note!

As a result of the *Journal-American's* exposé, some
small New York finance companies and auto dealers are
facing proceedings to revoke their licenses. Obviously,
reputable companies don't engage in such sharp practices. These rackets are worked mainly in populous communities where there are lots of semi-literate people to
victimize—although the victims are not always semi-
literate by any means.

The *Journal-American* unearthed a companion racket
in repair charges by "trap garages." You take your car in
for repairs. The garage manager is so breezy and friendly
you don't get an estimate in writing. When you come back
for your car you get a jolt to the solar plexus. Instead of
the $50 you expect, the bill is $600! And you have signed
in blank a financing agreement for the cost of the repairs.
You are stuck and if you don't pay, your car is seized and
sold at auction legally. The New York City licensing authorities started proceedings to padlock several garages
on the strength of the *Journal-American* stories.

Not keeping your wits about you when buying a used car is like a pitcher getting careless with Mickey Mantle at the plate.

So, bear in mind . . .

Too big a car, or too small a car, are both things to avoid.

A used car is a better financial proposition than is a new one.

It is cheaper to drive the same car for years. Trade-ins are relatively expensive; but a heavily used car should be traded in.

Jalopies have their uses, and can be money savers.

Financing a car varies in cost from city to city.

Watch out for: criminal and near-criminal auto dealers and auto loans, the "hidden load" contract, three-year collision policies.

15. Other Insurance

Nowadays the groom and often the bride as well, have Blue Cross Hospital Insurance, a medical policy and perhaps a major medical policy when they marry. *A major medical policy* is one that takes care of big hospital and medical expenses when benefits from Blue Cross and an ordinary medical policy are used up for a single illness. Most medical and hospitalization insurance is arranged and determined by negotiations between you and your employer or the employer and the union to which you belong.

If you are one of the comparatively few Americans who do not fall into one of these groups, you can buy comparable benefits in the same groups through any good life insurance agent or broker. So we need not go into great detail about medical and hospital insurance in this book except to recommend that everybody buy it. It is the first kind of insurance most people buy. The next is likely to be *automobile liability insurance*. And when you get a home of your own, you will buy *fire insurance,* perhaps a *comprehensive home insurance* policy, and you will need some kind of *general liability insurance*.

As in buying life insurance, the best person to buy all kinds of fire and casualty insurance from is a sound professional agent. The salesman for the individual company is too often a mere order taker and, at the best, he knows only his own company's policies and business. He is interested in pushing these and often does not have the time to consider your needs carefully. This results in a great deal of wasted money on the part of buyers of all types of insurance.

I would like to have just 10 per cent of the money that is wasted in about half of any business day on unnecessary or unwisely purchased insurance in the United States. Let's take our friend Joe Baltimore again. Joe goes to an insurance "store" and buys a minimum automobile liability policy from a salesman. Then a few months later Joe gets involved in a four-car crash and gets sued for $90,000.

Now, in a trial of an accident case, you are not allowed to disclose in court how much insurance you have— that's not allowed as it may influence the jury. So the jury brings in a verdict against Joe of $75,000. He has only $20,000 insurance and he can be garnisheed for the remaining $55,000 for the rest of his life, unless he goes into bankruptcy. It is a cinch Joe will not be able to sleep well for many years to come. Adequate protection would have cost Joe only about $17.00. Also for only about $16.00, he could have had additional protection for the $7,000 in medical bills for his own family.

When you buy automobile insurance you need to consider not only the least you can get by with, but medical protection for your family, property damage to your car and to other cars. There is also fire and theft insurance —and something called the uninsured interest clause, also called the family protection clause. This is a relatively cheap item which enables you to collect from your own insurance company if you are struck by a car driven by an uninsured driver.

In three or four states, automobile liability insurance is compulsory and to drive without it is a serious offense. To drive without adequate insurance anywhere is morally reprehensible and extremely irresponsible. The uninsured driver nowadays incurs a social stigma.

Once you get your auto insurance you must drive carefully to keep it, particularly if you live in one of the more populous states. If you are involved in an accident for which you file a claim, and if you are in any degree to blame, your rate will go up sharply the following year.

You have doubtless seen and heard many advertisements offering to save you substantial sums on automobile insurance. Some of these ads are true, others are very misleading. And in buying automobile insurance, the cheapest rate is not certain to be the best buy. There is a large difference in the services rendered to policyholders by the various companies, both in the matter of adjusting claims and in taking a fair attitude about continuing your insurance after an accident. Some companies will take weeks to settle a claim, perhaps leaving the unfortunate motorists without the use of their cars meanwhile. Other companies investigate and pay claims very quickly.

Some companies will refuse to renew your liability insurance for what may seem to you very inconsequential reasons. When this happens, the chances are you will be thrown into the *assigned risk pool*. That means your account is assigned to a company, at least theoretically against its will. In the assigned risk pool, you can only get the minimum amount of liability insurance, the so-called $10,000 to $20,000 policy, and at greatly increased rates. The better companies are reluctant to throw a policyholder into the assigned risk pool except for substantial cause.

The high cost of automobile insurance has become a national scandal in the United States. The Insurance Information Institute says the companies lost four cents on every dollar of premium they took in on it in 1962. Yet the rates are very burdensome and can amount to several hundred dollars a year on your car in New York City.

Personally, I think the blame for the high cost of auto insurance must be shared by auto owners, by unscrupulous garage operators, attorneys and politicians, and to a considerable extent by the insurance companies themselves.

The car owner is to blame because he still is not sufficiently aware of what a deadly, shiny weapon the Detroit factory has sold him. He doesn't educate himself about how easy it is to kill and maim with his car. Some unscrupulous garage men are perhaps the biggest single culprits. Their estimates and bills for repair jobs to be paid for by insurance companies are uniformly and outrageously inflated. Often, they even offer the car owner cash to present an inflated estimate to the insurance company.

Unscrupulous lawyers obtain personal injury judgments running into hundreds of thousands of dollars in automobile accident cases. The claims are often grossly inflated or even outright swindles based on fraudulent testimony.

The insurance companies are guilty because the supervision of their claim adjusting systems is lackadaisical and unbusinesslike. It is often done on a commission basis. The bigger the claim, the more the adjuster is paid. Why should he try to hold claims down? Nor have either the casualty insurance companies or life insurance companies carried out any very effective educational campaigns to make the public understand the necessity of cutting down auto accidents. All the companies do is yell for law enforcement. They do not engage in effective driver education.

The politicians are guilty because they completely condone perpetuation of the licensing to drive of a multitude of people who should be forbidden to drive for physical, mental or emotional reasons. There is much dispute as to the major cause of our high auto accident rate. Personally I think physical and emotional disabilities on the part of motorists deserve more attention as a major cause than they get. If this is true, then we are probably putting too much emphasis on point systems in figuring auto insurance rates.

On the subject of emotions and the car, I'd advise wives not to argue with their husbands while they are driving. An angry man is very dangerous at the wheel.

When you buy your first house, there is a good chance the mortgage company will put the insurance policy on it. The company will be interested in protecting its loan. Your insurance agent may very well be able to put a better policy on the house that will protect you against more hazards and perhaps save you considerable money. *It is pointless to insure your house for more than its worth.* No insurance company will pay you $50,000 for a $25,000 house that burns down no matter how much premium you have paid on it.

On the other hand, there is a clause in all fire- and material-damage policies, the co-insurance clause, which in effect says *you must carry adequate insurance in order to collect full insurance on any loss.* Adequate insurance is figured at 80 per cent of the appraised value of the house.

So if your house is worth $10,000, don't try to get away with insuring it for only $4,000, hoping it will never burn down; if you do have a $4,000 loss and the adjustor determines you were only half-covered, you won't get the $4,000, you'll only get $2,000. So on a house worth $10,000, you are obligated to carry $8,000 insurance, and that is what the mortgage companies would put on such a house. But contrary to what some people imagine, you can insure the house for the full $10,000, if it is worth that, and collect the whole sum if there is a total loss.

You can depend on your mortgage company, usually, to request you to increase your insurance as the value of your property goes up. The mortgage company wants to keep the property insured for 80 per cent of its value, so it will not be risking a loss under the coinsurance clause.

Our old friend Joe Baltimore also owned a house. The mortgage company put a fire insurance policy on it. But the mortgage company didn't care a hoot about insuring Joe's dog, or if somebody fell down and broke his leg over Joe's rake on his sidewalk. It was up to Joe's insurance agent to think about these things and to remind him to buy an *all-inclusive homeowner's policy* that protected him against all of these things, including theft from his house and grounds, storm damage, and even the risk of his foundation being cracked by sewer blasting a block or two away. These comprehensive policies include liability that may even protect you in case someone is hurt while riding in your rowboat miles away from your house.

Liability insurance is extremely necessary, in large amounts, to doctors and people like that. Take the case of Dr. McVitamin who had been in practice about twelve years and had accumulated about a quarter of a million dollars, yet was very naive about insurance. He had only minimum policies on his two cars, and he had no liability insurance even though he had a swimming pool in his back yard. He had no adequate malpractice liability insurance. Then one day a very ill patient collapsed in Dr. McVitamin's office, stumbled against an X-ray machine, and fell down dead. In vain, Dr. McVitamin's lawyers argued that the patient probably would have died anyway. You never know what a judge and jury are going to say. In this country anybody can sue anybody any time —and, all too often, can succeed unjustly. With no liability insurance benefits of any kind, Dr. McVitamin is now paying off a $150,000 judgment to the widow of the man who fell against his X-ray machine. The tragedy of it is that *large liability policies are very reasonable.* Substantial business or professional men now can buy liability protection for up to a million dollars, very cheaply. The reason is that such policies normally have *deductible clauses ranging from $1,000 to $10,000.* The policy holder is protected by other policies on the smaller claims. That drastically reduces the rate of the special policy for big claims.

So, bear in mind . . .

Your best bet is to buy life insurance, and all insurance, from professional insurance agents.

The insurance you have may leave you unprotected in vital spots. For example, do you have comprehensive home insurance? Does your auto insurance have an uninsured driver clause, and does it cover fire, theft, medical protection for passengers, and property damage?

It's up to you to protect your auto insurance by driving carefully.

Don't waste money by overinsuring your house. The company will not pay more than it's worth. But, don't underinsure if you expect full payments from the company.

Doctors and other professional men may require liability insurance, which is not expensive for the coverage it provides.

16. You Should Buy Stocks

Comparatively early in your active career, you should start buying stocks.

Perhaps you will lose a little money buying stocks, although that is far from necessary. But even if you do, the experience will be worth something. It will teach you far more and, in the long run, will give you more satisfaction than money you lose (or win) playing poker or bridge, shooting dice or going to the racetrack.

Not that buying stocks ought to be regarded as gambling. "Playing the market" without expert advice, frequently getting in and out of stocks held on big margin, paying brokers' commissions on each end of every deal, and often taking comparatively big losses and small profits, is gambling; it is not even speculating. I don't propose that any young couple deliberately squander money that way.

Why then do I suggest that young people start to buy stocks? For three reasons:

1. Stocks are the basic method by which wealth is accumulated in the United States.

2. They are the one great protection against inflation.

3. Widely spread ownership of stocks unquestionably is the answer of Western free society (not only in the overwhelmingly "capitalist" United States but in semi-socialist Britain and Continental Europe as well) to Communist economic dogma. This applies particularly where workers own shares in the companies in which they are employed.

Let's consider the third proposition first. It's the least

understood, yet it is the most important of the three, and it represents "the wave of the future" about which political prophets like to talk.

The Communists, who in their own jargon refer to their economic systems as "socialism," claim that under this system, the people own and control the means of production, distribution, and financing directly.

But who does control the economy of the Soviet Union? —or of Red China?

Answer: The Communist Party.

For many years, the Communist Party in the Soviet Union numbered fewer than two million people. There is reason to suppose it numbers much fewer than ten million today out of a population of well over two hundred million. But it is tightly controlled. Only a few hundred thousand members—perhaps only 150 thousand have any real say-so in party affairs. But these people really control everything in the Soviet Union: the economy, the courts, the military, education, religion, social customs, morality—absolutely everything.

Who owns and controls the economy of the United States?

Books have been written over the years claiming that fifty families or four hundred families control the economic life of our country.

And to be candid, there have been eras when the control and ownership of much of our industry, finance and distribution seemed remarkably concentrated.

Yet the roster of the rich families shifts endlessly and bewilderingly, like the patterns of the brilliant bits of colored glass in a kaleidoscope. The number of wealthy families multiplies, too, while we see many other rich families fall apart and lose what they have; the old English maxim "shirt sleeves to shirt sleeves in three generations" seems as true today as in the nineteenth century.

Now, let's take a look at such facts and figures as we

have on the subject. The New York Stock Exchange has estimated that something over 16 million Americans, out of a population of around 190 million, own voting stocks in listed companies. On the basis of that figure alone, at least twice as many Americans as Soviet citizens, and perhaps many times as many, have a direct ownership and voting voice in the control of their country's economy.

Only about 2,500 companies are listed on the two big stock exchanges in New York, a handful more on the Midwest Exchange in Chicago and on the San Francisco Exchange. Then there are another two thousand or so public companies whose stocks are quoted regularly on the over-the-counter market.

But more than 200,000 corporations file income tax returns annually with the United States Treasury!

A few thousand of these are wholly owned subsidiaries of the big listed corporations, so they have no individual stockholders of their own. But it's safe to say that there are upwards of 180,000 private business corporations in the United States, each having from three hundred to several hundred stockholders. Many of these stockholders in private corporations are the same people who own shares in the public companies. So there is no way of telling how many Americans own common stocks and thereby have a voting voice and direct share in the ownership of the economy of our country. But we do know that the number is many, many times the number of upper-echelon Communist Party members who have a real voting say in how the economy of Russia or Red China is run. And, every American citizen has a direct vote in the political and social rule of the country.

We also know the proportion of Americans who have such a voice is increasing rapidly. It is much easier to see the working out of this dramatic and vital trend in our economy and society when we reduce it to the company level.

Within the memory of some living Americans, there was not one big corporation in our country that did not have a single family or dominant group at the top. J. P. Morgan controlled U.S. Steel after buying out Andy Carnegie. First Cliff Durant, then the DuPont family, controlled General Motors. Alexander Graham Bell and a small group of bankers controlled the Bell Telephone system.

Today, there must be much more than one million stockholders in the Bell Telephone system—and even the hugest institutional owner, such as a giant life insurance company, hasn't as much as one-half of 1 per cent of the shares. The federal courts have forced the DuPonts to start selling off their $3 billion stake in General Motors, but even before the court decision was handed down after a long legal battle, GM had grown until it had almost one million stockholders and DuPont's big chunk of the stock no longer was sufficient to control the company.

Of course most companies, even those with more than $100 million a year in sales, still do have a dominant control group of sorts, but the heads that wear the crowns lie uneasy; they know control can be wrested from them in a proxy battle. This type of struggle hinges, in part, on money to go into the market to buy voting shares; but more important are direct appeals for the votes of the small shareholders—much like the appeals the management of a city or a county or a candidate for Congress must make to voters in the political lists.

The annual elections of directors of some of our biggest corporations are now starting to take on the importance in this country of the elections of governors and mayors.

If you don't believe that, attend the annual meeting of Standard Oil Company (New Jersey), or of Pan-American World Airways, and observe the deference with which big league presidents like Monroe Rathbone of Jersey, or

Juan Trippe of Pan-Am, treat small stockholders who get up and demand to be heard, perhaps to ask naive questions or to make naive or snide remarks. Notice the amount of time and money spent to prepare for the meeting and the trouble taken to get a big turnout of shareholders.

Of course, there's more to it than just running for office; after all, the running for office isn't a critical matter as yet. In most companies there still is a control group, and in those where there isn't the stockholders have no incentive to rock the boat and to kick the management out—so long as the company seems to be forging ahead or holding its own.

Stockholders also tend to be customers and the company with lots of stockholders who hang on to their shares can count on a big block of pre-sold business, year in and year out, other things being reasonable equal.

Possibly the biggest single reason for General Motors' present dominant position in the auto industry (along with making reliable cars) is that its army of stockholders has grown so enormously. Possibly, the failure of the Ford family to realize this factor and seek a wide-spread stock ownership for Ford was the main reason Ford lost its dominance, which once was relatively greater than GM's is today.

But whether it is motivated by sales appeal or by the desire of the directors and management to keep the goodwill of shareholders, or both, *the wooing of stockholders* and the effort to expand stock ownership in the country's private enterprise economy is probably the most important social phenomenon of the middle of the twentieth century and will continue to be so for some years.

It's a long, long road we have traveled since Jay Gould and Jim Fisk used to hold the annual meeting of the Erie Railroad on a boat in the middle of the East River so no other stockholders could get there and challenge their brazenly forged proxies. Curiously, the railroad industry remains the last citadel of the managerial arrogance, stupidity and inefficiency that treats stockholders with about as much consideration as most of us give to the house fly.

The proposition that *common stocks are the basic way of accumulating wealth* in this country is almost axiomatic. You cannot find a large fortune whose building blocks were not mainly common stocks. The "nut," or original stake, of course, rarely came from common stocks. It may have come from the professional fees of a doctor or a lawyer, the commissions of a successful salesman of commodities or life insurance, the growing salary of a brilliant manager, the royalties of a writer, or the big bonus from a fat part played by a good actor.

But the fortune grows out of common stocks. Other ways of investing money produce a steady income in the shape of interest and some speculative profit. Land, for example, sometimes produces remarkable profits over the years. But even land often is turned into common stocks. Stocks are the most volatile and the most expansible of investments. They are the sinews of a free enterprise society. They will work for the economy and for individuals under a semi-socialist system as well as under capitalism, so long as there is reasonable freedom to manage, and the people are allowed enough freedom to have the means and incentive to buy the goods industry produces.

The second proposition, that *common stocks are the one great protection against inflation,* is almost equally axiomatic. Of course, land, works of art, stocks of food, machinery, and some other material possessions go up in price sharply in periods of inflation, too. But, except in time of runaway inflation, these things are not so easily liquidated, or made use of to produce new capital or income, as are common stocks.

In the next chapter, I will get down to cases, describe stocks briefly and tell my own ideas about the right way to invest money in stocks.

So, bear in mind . . .

Moderate, early buying of stocks is the best way to learn the art of stock investment.

Common stocks are the best way to accumulate wealth, protect yourself against inflation, and they are the basis of a free economy.

The 16 million Americans who own stocks are contributing to, and sharing in the control of, their country's economy.

Stockholders tend to be customers—and, their votes are often essential in intra-company disputes. So, the stockholder is an important man.

17. How to Buy Stocks

There are many kinds of stocks: *Preferred stocks,* for example. These bear a fixed dividend rate in percentage of par value or as a flat sum. These dividends must be paid by the company *before* any dividends can be paid on common stock, hence the name preferred.

Some preferred stocks, most in fact, are cumulative; that is, if the dividend is not earned and paid in full in any year, it remains as a debt (like the interest on a bond or a note), but a company cannot be thrown into bankruptcy because of arrears on preferred stock dividends; *dividends are payable only when earned.*

Many preferred stocks are *convertible* into common stock at a given period and a definite price. That may make them especially desirable.

Preferred stocks may or may not have voting rights; in past eras, they usually did not, and sometimes they had fixed dividend rates as high as 7 per cent. Four to 5 per cent is more common nowadays, and preferred stocks have voting rights more often than not.

Preferred stocks do not usually benefit from stock dividends or stock splits, or from the distribution of capital assets when a company grows or makes a fat deal. So they are not the building blocks of a fortune as common stocks are. They are definitely for production of income although, in a fast growing company, a convertible preferred stock may bring its holder a good share in the company's growth.

A company may have several issues of preferred, at

different dividend rates, outstanding; but, the total of the preferred stock normally is considerably less than of the common stock. Moreover, the company may retain the right to *retire* the preferred stock if paying the dividends on it becomes burdensome. Such retirements are frequent.

Some companies have several classes of common stock. Sometimes there is a good reason for this, one class is stock held in reserve; this is authorized, but unissued, stock for buying other companies or making deals when an opportunity comes up. But sometimes the reason is bad; for example, the Securities and Exchange Commission has been very critical of some public real estate investment companies for putting the entire voting power in a separate class of common stock owned by the management. This special common stock draws no dividends but rules the company. The SEC's stern criticism has caused some companies to retire this special stock and to give the investors a normal voice in the affairs of the company.

Years ago, when only the rich bought stocks, the normal par value of common stocks was $100 a share. Since 100 shares is the trading unit on the big stock exchanges, that meant the minimum deal that could be handled on the floor was $5,000 to $15,000, assuming the *market value* of $100 par stocks ranged from around $50 to $150. As proof of the wide interest of companies in getting many stockholders, nearly all new stock issues nowadays are in shares with no par value or with nominal par values of $1 to $10, and nearly all the big blue chip stocks have been split up more than once. Of course some of them have gone back up again to way over $100 a share after each split because the company was doing so well.

Common stocks of public companies are classified in many ways. First, they divide into Listed and Unlisted (or Over-the-Counter stocks). Listed stocks are those traded every day on the big stock exchanges. The exchanges require that the companies have so many thousand stockholders and so many hundred thousand shares in the hands of the public and, on the New York Stock Exchange, there is a substantial minimum amount of sales a company must report to keep its listing.

Listed stocks can be bought quickly at narrow price swings and they can be bought *on margin.* Margin means your stockbroker lends you money to enable you to buy more stock. The legal maximum amount the broker can lend you is fixed by the Federal Reserve Board. It is nowadays never more than 30 per cent of the market value of the stock. If you buy stocks on margin, you must pay the broker interest on the margin loan. If the stock you are carrying on margin goes down sharply, the broker will call on you for more cash (margin) to reduce the loan. If you can't supply it and the price keeps on going down, the broker will sell the stock and reimburse himself, and you have lost much of your investment. Carrying a lot of stocks on margin is dangerous speculation for anyone without large reserves of cash. In the autumn of 1929, many great fortunes were wiped out that way in a single month.

In the May, 1962, collapse of the stock market, there were some spectacular personal losses in the same manner.

Common stocks also are classified by business groups. Averages and statistics are kept for the industrials, the public utilities and the railways. These indices, the Dow-Jones averages, the Standard & Poor's Index of 500 Stocks, and the Alfred M. Best Life Insurance Stock Index are good indicators of the trend of market, but many people who invest or who "play the market" attach far too much importance to them. You can't make money very fast if you go by averages. Money is made in what security men call "growth stocks" and "special situations."

Unlisted stocks are traded on a bid-and-asked basis through over-the-counter brokers. It is a much slower process and has much wider price swings. There are many hundreds of excellent stocks in the over-the-counter market and far more fortunes are made there than on the exchange floors. But there are also thousands of unwise promotions, speculations, and some outright swindles among the stocks in the over-the-counter market. There also are promotions and speculations among *listed* stocks and occasionally an outright swindle occurs in the securities of a listed company in spite of the vigilance of the exchanges.

But the most important way in which common stocks are classified is into "income" and "growth" stocks. *Income stocks* are those that yield a relatively high income in proportion to market price.

Growth stocks normally do not yield a big income or any income. But the companies that issue them give *stock* dividends, split the stock, or simply grow very fast while plowing their earnings back into the company so that the *potential or book value* of the stock gets very high. The stocks of some life insurance companies are outstanding examples of growth stocks. There are a number of life insurance companies in which a $10,000 investment around 1950 grew to $250,000 or even to $400,000 within ten years—even though the company paid almost no cash dividends during that time.

But there are many good growth stocks among industrials and utilities, too. International Business Machines Company has had an outstanding record among industrial growth stocks in the past twenty-five years or so.

Some of our giant companies virtually qualify on their past records as both income and growth stocks: General Motors for example. But such companies now must be regarded as mature companies and primarily as income stocks. In past years they grew fantastically while paying out large cash dividends at the same time.

In addition to being the building blocks of personal fortunes, growth stocks can provide income at substantial savings under our present Federal tax system. Remember that cash dividends are income and are taxable at full income rates except for minor credits. But *stock* dividends are not income; they are appreciation of capital. So is any increase in the market value of a stock you own. Therefore, the profit on the stock is a capital gain under the tax laws and is not taxable *until you sell the stock.* And then it is taxable only to the maximum capital gains rate of 25 per cent even though the rest of your income puts you in a higher tax bracket, provided you hold the stock for more than six months. So you may reap a better income in the long run from a growth stock by selling some of the shares from time to time than you could hope to reap from stocks paying big cash dividends.

Having decided you are going to invest in common stocks, how do you go about it? Many people try to do it on their own. They buy the *Wall Street Journal,* and read it every day. They subscribe to a weekly financial magazine or to one of the advertised investor's services. If you have a natural knack for it and if you have the time to devote to it, you may do fairly well in this manner.

But the chances are that you won't have the time to devote to it and you won't have a natural knack for it; in fact, unless you are in a business that naturally trains you for investing in stocks, the chances are that, the more skilled and more successful you are in your profession or business, the less likely you are to have the time, patience and aptitude to be a stock market investor on your own.

So you need professional advice. How do you get it?

Even with hundreds of brokers, friends, and investor's services eager to advise you, the question is not easy to answer unless you are rich and have no urgent need to augment your income and aren't particularly anxious for your fortune to grow at any great rate; in that case you go to the trust department of a good bank and perhaps, in addition, get the services of one of the biggest and most expensive investor counseling firms in New York—and leave everything up to them.

If, like most people, you have only a small stake and are struggling to get a start, it's not easy to get safe advice, much less advice that will really make your stake grow.

Many of the investor's advisory services that advertise constantly are not on the up-and-up; the so-called advisers are actually toting and unloading stocks for themselves or their financial backers on their unwary clients. Even supposedly reputable firms have been caught red-handed in such activities in recent years, and even big banks have been involved on the fringes of such shenanigans—witness the $50-million swindles of Lowell M. Birrell, a scandal that wrecked more than one brokerage house and has resulted in enormous law suits against the American Stock Exchange, banks and others accused of carelessness.

And, some of the thoroughly legitimate investment counseling houses are too expensive for the small investor, or their viewpoint is attuned only to the very conservative needs of the big investor; they will safeguard your $5,000 for you, but they are psychologically incapable of making it grow. They are afraid of "special situations" and are temperamentally inclined to dismiss them as dangerous speculations—until someday they learn some astute investors have exploited such situations to run $5,000 up to $150,000 or more in ten years.

As for the local branch manager of a Wall Street house or the salesman who used to be called a customer's man but nowadays is called a *registered representative* or an *account executive,* well, *his job is to sell stocks,* not to make money for you, the propaganda of the public relations departments of the stock exchanges and of the big Wall Street houses to the contrary, notwithstanding. It is true that the Wall Street community has made a big effort in recent years to improve the qualifications of sales personnel but, still, mighty few of them are really well trained or able to give you any clear advisory program, only an occasional tip that may backfire disastrously.

You do need the services of a stockbroker to buy stocks. In most cities you must deal with a branch of one of the big chain Wall Street houses; there isn't anyone else. If you live close to one of the bigger cities, you may be able to get the services of a good smaller brokerage house where a partner in the firm might take an interest in you and give you somewhat more personal service.

You will be in a better position, though, if you can find a really first-rate investment counselor. Such a man is worth his weight in gold. You should choose an investment counselor on a strictly professional basis. Don't give your investment business to some guy because he happens to be your wife's cousin; who, in his right mind, wants his wife's cousin to know his investment secrets anyway?

And don't pick a chap who advertises himself as an investment counselor because he happens to belong to your church or plays golf with you; you're liable to find he's out to club you. In fact, the chances are you will be better off with an investment counselor you have not met on a social basis. I know that's going to sound like rank heresy to many of my confreres in the security business. Things have been done—or misdone—the other way for, lo, these many years.

Investigate the professional qualifications of your prospective investment counselor. Try to talk to a couple of his clients and get specific information about what he has accomplished for them.

Once you have found the man, trust him as you trust your doctor. He can help you only if you take his medicine.

Give him your loyalty, too. His personal share of the fees his firm is going to make out of your account is meager enough; so, if you eat into his time and energy only to give some of your investment business to someone else, you are cheating him and defeating your own purpose because he, naturally, will lose interest in your problems. You don't go to three doctors for one ordinary tummyache or hire three lawyers to write the same will.

But suppose you want to get started investing in stocks in a small way while you are hunting for a good investment counselor, what then? There are a few rules that are helpful.

1. Don't worry if the first stock you buy goes down a little, especially if it is an income stock. After all, you bought this particular stock to get the 40-cents-a-share quarterly dividend. So long as you get the 40 cents regularly it doesn't matter a damn to you whether the stock is selling for $19 or $17 or $21—it's a good buy at any of those prices.

2. Invest a regular amount each month or each quarter. Add all the dividends you collect to your investment fund.

3. Diversify your holdings as steadily as you can. It may pay you to buy some stocks on margin, just to get some diversity in your holdings.

But what kind of stocks should you buy?

Perhaps public utility stocks are about the best combination of income yield and growth possibilities for the novice investor. The energy requirements of the country are growing at a remarkable rate, so the electric power and gas utility business hardly has any place to go but up.

The food processing and distribution industry is another good one that has to grow, and is generally profitable in all times. Unfortunately, many excellent companies in this field are closely held with not much stock available. But the records of the food industry shares that are available are generally good.

I mentioned *life insurance company* stocks, with which I have a great familiarity, as the most astonishing growth stocks. They have been for many years. Although there are many sleepy life insurance companies that do not grow, the shares as a group have outperformed industrials, utilities and rails on the exchanges and the so-called "glamour stocks" on the over-the-counter market by a wide margin.* Life insurance company stocks are unlisted, so they cannot be bought on margin; they pay very small *cash* dividends or no cash dividends, but the good companies pay frequent stock dividends and split their stocks often.

The number of stockbrokers who know life insurance company stocks is infinitesimal; many investment counselors don't know them well either, but a good investment counselor may know where to turn to get advice about life insurance stocks.

During the great stock market boom after World War II that was climaxed by the May, 1962, collapse, we heard a great deal about "glamor stocks," particularly the stocks of electronics companies. The boom in the electronics industry, of course, was legitimate, based on remarkable new technology and solid growth. But the boom in electronics "glamor stocks" had a horribly seamy side. Shares of hundreds of new electronics companies were floated on the over-the-counter market. The gullible public was so eager to buy any new stock that had the label "electronic" that each new issue jumped in value as soon as the underwriters had unloaded it. Now, many of these companies had, as an SEC report said, "no real business except the production of their own securities." They were hitchhiking on the booming rise in the shares of some of the big, legitimate electronics manufacturers. The inevitable happened; the electronics stocks lost their glamor and spearheaded the May, 1962, collapse. There was a lot of plain trickery in the promotion of many of these stocks.

I go into this in order to emphasize as strongly as I can that a *"glamor stock"* is not a "special situation." Many naive people are dazzled by "glamor stocks." They

* See *Life Insurance Stocks, The Modern Gold Rush,* by Arthur Milton, The Citadel Press, New York, 1963.

think because a stock has come up rapidly, it will keep on going up. What they don't realize is that *the legitimate glamor stock is a former "special situation" that no longer is special!* The stock has *had* its biggest rise, and now has become a normal investment with its natural limitations.

That brings up an important corrolary of the maxim that fortunes are made in the stock market mainly in "special situations"; the corrolary is that you cannot run with the herd and make money. You have to buy when the herd is selling to get a low price and you have to sell when the herd is eager to buy in order to get a good price —in the meantime, you must know how to watch and wait and go along with the herd until the right moment to sell or buy.

There are bound to be lots of genuine *special situations* in stocks around the country that will make fortunes for some people. But when we read that $10,000 invested in International Business Machines Company had grown to around $250,000 ten years later, we must ask ourselves, to be honest, "Who foresaw it?"

Very few people foresaw it, even within the company. The truth is that *hardly anybody, even experts, can recognize a true special situation in advance.* And most people who stumble into a special situation climb out in a hurry as soon as they have made a little profit. How many people, do you suppose, bought IBM, then sold it, then bought it again, then sold again, during those ten years of its spectacular growth? They got out with small profits and sometimes even with losses, for, like all glamor stocks, IBM has had wide price swings—sometimes $15 to $25 a share in a single day.

"Miss Special Situation" is not likely to give you the eye if you play the field, as some speculators seem to imagine.

That's as naive a way to go about it as putting $2 on the nose of every nag in a six-horse race at Aqueduct.

The chances of the winning $2 ticket paying enough to return a real profit on the $12 outlay are negligible; you're pretty sure to lose.

Yet whenever there's a boom in some new industry and a lot of stocks of new companies are floated, a host of investors rush to buy small blocs of stock in a number of the companies, hoping to snare the one stock that will pay off on the long haul.

Financial Editor Leslie Gould of the New York *Journal-American* published in August, 1963, a revealing article about what happened to the people who rushed into the market to buy new stocks floated during the bowling boom of 1959 and 1960.

Millions were invested in new publicly-owned chains of bowling centers. The stocks were snapped up as fast as they came out and most of them rose rapidly on the over-the-counter or the American Stock Exchange. So did the shares of two big listed companies that make automatic bowling equipment.

But the insiders (who make a habit of this sort of operation) sold the new bowling center stocks before the peak of the rise, *leaving the suckers to hold the bag*.

And the bag really emptied.

Long before August, 1963, Gould showed, the shares of the two big listed companies that make automatic bowling equipment were drastically deflated. As for the new stocks of a score of bowling alley chains, only one had retained any semblance of substantial value and it was depressed. One stock floated at $6 a share had risen as high as $36.50 and then plunged to 10 cents. Another, offered originally at $3, went up to $34 but was selling for 50 cents in August, 1963. Half of the others had dropped to less than $1 a share from highs of $7 to above $25!

Gould wrote that it was obvious that many millions of dollars were lost by naive investors in these bowling alley promotions. Who got the money? The bowling promoters got some of it but, generally speaking, they were not the culprits. As often as not, they were the victims of their own over optimism. *The loot went to the smart fast buck operators in Wall Street,* the sharp insiders who knew how to get the stocks at the original offering price, then unload them near the peak of the rise to the gullible "investors" who were trying to find a winner by "playing the field."

It is not only in the lucky special situation that patience is the prime requirement for success in investing in stocks. Bank trust officers, investment counselors and estate planners constantly warn that it takes time to invest successfully in stocks. My own idea about it is: "The patient investor gets compounded—the impatient investor gets confounded."

So you need a regular pattern and program to follow.

But how well can you hope to do?

Obviously you can hope to do better if you have a lump-sum nest egg of a few thousand dollars than if you have to save up a stake at, say $25 a month, for you can start getting income and growth at once on the lump sum if you invest it successfully. Accumulating enough capital at $25 a month to show results takes time. You can't even start investing until you have saved the first $600 or so, and that takes two years.

Unfortunately, some people who try to tell you how well you can do, hold out the prospect of doing as well as the stocks in the Dow-Jones industrial average. But you can't invest that way; it could cost far too much money to buy odd lots of shares in all the stocks in the Dow-Jones average; so, to base your expectations on the past performances of the Dow-Jones average (or any other average) seems to me quite illusory.

Of course, it is possible that you might do better than the Dow-Jones industrial average; if so, you are either very skillful or very lucky. Chances are, I think, much against doing that well.

If you had been investing $25 a month and had accumulated dividends in common stocks between 1944 and 1953, and had succeeded in doing as well as the Dow-Jones industrial average, your three thousand dollars would have doubled in that period. If you take the ten years from 1952 through 1961, the results would have been better and it probably would have been easier then to do as well as the Dow-Jones average.

But the really significant thing is that, in either case, your gains would have begun to compound *after the completion of the first 10 years*. Your $6,000 accumulation, as of January 1, 1953, would have grown to $12,000 as of January 1, 1956, if you had kept the program up and continued to do as well as the Dow-Jones average. Remember, I'm not saying you would have done that well.

And the same re-doubling of your stake might well have occurred between 1961 and 1964 in spite of the clobbering you would have taken in the May 28, 1962, collapse, if you had kept your program up wisely.

There is nothing new about all this. The elder John D. Rockefeller used to beg people to save money to buy common stocks. He pointed out that the way this country was growing, stocks on the average had to go up, and, therefore, the patient investor had to come out on top if he adopted a sensible program and stuck to it.

There is another and easier (and more controversial) way of investing in stocks: *Mutual Funds*. I fancy readers have been wondering when I was going to get around to this great phenomenon. In the mutual fund you don't buy stocks directly, you buy shares in a fund managed by a company. You pay the company an original fee of about 8 per cent, then, an annual management fee of about one-half of 1 per cent.

Most mutual funds are growth funds, although a few

are operated to produce income for the shareholders. Some of them specialize, putting up to 75 per cent of their funds in a particular type of security. As might be expected, mutual funds specializing in life insurance stocks have had an outstanding growth record.

In at least one important respect, the mutual fund industry's great growth in the past dozen years (actually, the mutual fund idea is around forty years old) has been a tremendous success. Mutual funds have persuaded an enormous number of Americans to invest money in the country's industry. Perhaps $15 billion, or roughly half of the current assets of the mutual funds, is new money poured into stocks of industry by small investors. That is of great importance and benefit to all of us.

But the question of how successful mutual funds have been for the small investor is more difficult to answer. Right off the bat, we can give one important answer though—it is relatively safe. You would have to be pretty stupid to lose your money in mutual fund shares. Off hand, I can't think of a way to do it. But the big question is, can you make any money buying mutual fund shares?

The advertising of the mutual fund companies and the glowing prospects held out by many of their salesmen sound wonderful. But not everybody is convinced. Many investment counselors say they frequently find clients who have been paying substantial funds into mutual funds for some years and have little to show for their money. They have not received any cash dividends to speak of, and the asset value of their shares hasn't gone up appreciably. They are not even as well off as if they had paid their $40 to $200 a month into a savings deposit at 4¾ per cent compounded quarterly in a California savings bank.

I certainly don't want to give the impression that it is true of all mutual funds, or even is typical—but I personally have seen it happen a number of times.

But I also have seen examples of mutual fund programs, persisted in for ten years or longer, that produced good results—a pay-in of $3,000 built up to $10,000, for example. What it boils down to is, the mutual fund is a slow starter but does pretty well for the long pull for the investor who cannot afford the services of an investment counselor and cannot invest wisely on his own—but I can think of no way in which mutual funds can make you rich. Investing in stocks on your own with a good counselor can make you rich—with luck. Of course, you might not have the luck.

The Wharton School of Finance of the University of Pennsylvania currently is making a long-range study of the mutual fund industry for the federal government, from the point of view of the individual investor. A report on the first phase of the study already has been published and it was not flattering to the industry. In essence, the Wharton professors said mutual funds had done no better by the small investor than he could have done on his own by watching the Dow-Jones averages and following them. This obvious boner by the Wharton professors incensed the officers of the Investment Company Institute, to which many mutual funds belong. They pointed out, just as I have in this chapter, that the small investor can't possibly follow the Dow-Jones averages in making investments and has little chance of doing as well as the Dow-Jones averages on his own. So if the mutual funds were keeping up with or almost keeping up with the Dow-Jones index, the Institute felt they were doing pretty well.

But some investment counselors may do much better.

So, BEAR IN MIND . . .

Don't buy a stock until you are familiar with the many types and classes that are offered. Each classification of stock has its uses, but know what you are buying.

Buying on margin is a useful method, but it has its

dangers, and you pay interest on the money you are using for margin.

You do need professional advice in this field. Be careful where you seek it. A broker's representative is a salesman; he is not the man to advise you.

Special situation stocks are fine, if you can find them.

Glamor stocks are yesterday's special situation stocks, and they are no bargain.

Find a good investment counselor—and listen to what he says.

Mutual funds are all right—if you can't invest wisely on your own.

18. Bonds and Debentures

People with a substantial bit of money who, for reasons of health or temperament, don't want to invest in stocks or operate a business usually buy bonds or debentures.

A bond is a promise to pay the principal and interest on a loan. A first mortgage bond is backed by a first mortgage on the assets of a corporation after wages, mechanic's liens and tax claims are satisfied.

A debenture is also a certificate of a share in a loan, but it is an unsecured bond because it is not, in general, backed by a specific collateral. In case of liquidation of the company, it takes its place somewhere near the head of the general creditors after wages, mechanic's liens, taxes and secured bondholders have been satisfied.

A convertible debenture is a type of security that has become very popular in recent years; *it can be traded in* at the holder's option, at a definite time and at a definite price, for common stock in the company. Often the stock goes up or is split so much after the convertible is issued that the convertible will buy the stock at a huge bargain. That naturally makes the convertible debenture very valuable and its price goes very high on the bond market.

Tax exempts are bonds issued by states, counties, cities and school, water, drainage, and sewer districts and other local government agencies, and by some state universities. The Federal government issued tax-exempt bonds until the time of President Franklin D. Roosevelt. But so many wealthy people put nearly all their money in tax-exempt bonds, and thereby escaped paying their fair share of the cost of running the federal government, that it became a national scandal; so, Congress put a stop to federal tax exempts. The interest on all federal loans, even the Series E savings bonds, now is taxable.

Congress wanted to start taxing the interest on state and municipal bonds, too, but the federal courts said the Constitution does not give it that power, so local governments still issue tax exempts. Without tax exemption, states and local governments would have to pay much higher interest on the money they borrow to build schools, roads, and to finance other local needs. Interest on tax-exempt bonds is low—2 per cent is good.

Nor is their safety record particularly good; they nearly always get paid off at par, ultimately—but sometimes they go into default and depreciate until their market value is very low (perhaps 25 or 30 cents on the dollar) for considerable periods. And, remember, a municipality cannot be liquidated to satisfy the claims of its creditors. When a corporation fails to meet its bond interest, it may be put in bankruptcy and, if necessary, liquidated to meet the claims of bondholders—but the owners of tax-exempt state and municipal bonds just have to wait many years until the state or municipality gets on its feet again.

There is one type of *railway bond* called the *income bond* which provides that the interest must be paid only if the railroad earns it that year. The only difference between an income bond and stock, thus, is that the income bond ultimately must be redeemed by the railroad at par. Some tax-exempts called *"revenue bonds"* are similar to railway income bonds in this respect.

The bond market is a vigorous and complicated affair *and is no place for the naive.* You need expert advice in buying bonds or you may find yourself taking greater risks than you would in running a business or buying stocks. Since many people think the mere word "bond" implies great safety, it's well to emphasize this point. It is possible that as much or more money has been lost by people who bought bad bonds than by people who bought bad stocks. What's worse, generally speaking, people who lose on bad bonds are less able to afford the loss than those who lose on stocks.

Foreign bonds have been a big source of loss to Americans in this century; but to be fair about it, American bonds, corporate municipals bonds and the share of the defeated Confederacy, were a huge source of loss to European investors in the nineteenth century. American investors lost many millions of dollars in European and Latin American government and corporate bonds floated in this country before World War I and during the high, wide and handsome 1920s.

However, the notion that bonds cannot result in much profit, only in income, is not strictly true. Skilled traders sometimes realize large long-term profits *by discovering special situations in bonds.* An example: One of the most famous and biggest hotels in Manhattan opened at the bottom of the Great Depression to very poor business. In no time, the bonds issued to finance its construction and operation fell to a bit over 10 cents on the dollar. But the hotel company managed to escape liquidation or having to refinance the bonds on a basis that would have cancelled them. Some smart traders bought up many of the bonds at the low prices. Eventually, the bonds were redeemed at par. The traders who bought them had a profit of 750 to 900 per cent, plus the interest accumulated on them over the years.

More often, though, when a company defaults for any length of time on bond interest, it goes through receivership and reorganization in bankruptcy, and a refinancing in which the principal value of the bonds is written down sharply.

So the notion that bonds *per se* are safer than stocks

or other types of investments is subject to many reservations.

Bonds and debentures are issued in denominations of $1,000 and $500 and, occasionally, in $100 packets. *The Treasury savings bonds* (issued in denominations of $25 and up) are really *discount bonds.* Instead of the government paying you interest on them, it sells you the bond at a 25 per cent discount and you get the interest in a lump sum when you cash the bond in.

The stated rate of interest (or, coupon rate, as it is called) is not the actual amount of income you get from a bond or a debenture. That depends on how much you paid for it; if you buy a 4 per cent bond for a quoted price of 80 (which means $800 for a $1,000 bond), you will be getting 5 per cent per annum *true* interest on your investment. But if you paid 110 for the bond, you would be getting only 3.6 per cent on your money.

When new bonds and debentures are issued, they frequently are sold at auction to the highest bidder. An underwriting syndicate of bond houses lands them at a price a little under par, as a rule, or at a little over par in the case of a very desirable issue. The underwriting syndicate then re-sells the bonds to investors at a slightly higher price. The actual yield to the investor has to be figured by dividing the retail price into the coupon interest rate.

Corporate bonds often are issued serially because the company wants to amortize the issue annually or every three to five years in installments. In such issues, the bonds that run for the longest period usually bear higher coupon interest rates than those that are to be redeemed early. That's to compensate for the fact that the holder must wait a much longer period to get his money back at par.

It's also well to remember that just because you buy a bond or a debenture with a nice fat interest yield, that's no sign you're going to be allowed to sit back and clip coupons and collect your interest year after year.

Somewhere in the fine print on the bond you will usually find a clause permitting the company or municipality that borrowed the money to issue new bonds at cheaper rates of interest after a certain period if the market goes down. *You may be required to accept the new bond —and less income.*

President Kennedy asked Congress to put an equalizing tax on foreign investments by Americans to preserve our balance of payments situation. Just before that, Mexico floated its first issue of bonds in the United States in 53 years—$25 million of them at a net yield to the American bond buyers of 7 per cent.

Only two days later, the State of Connecticut sold bonds in New York at a net interest cost of only 2.85 per cent. Why could Connecticut borrow so cheaply and why did Mexico have to pay so much—even though Mexico has good bank credit?

In the first place, *Connecticut's bonds are tax exempt* to American holders *and Mexico's are not.* But that's not the big reason. The big reason is that back in 1914, Mexico defaulted on her entire public debt during her period of revolutionary upheaval and ultimately settled the principal of about a quarter of billion dollars in bonded debt at 20 cents on the dollar, in addition to scaling down the interest charges.

A long term corporate bond—twenty to thirty years— may depreciate sharply in re-sale price even though interest payments are not in default during the middle period of its life. That's because the market for it may become thin even if it is an obligation of a well-known company; the market for the bond becomes thin because interest rates on bonds and debentures in general have gone up since it was issued, and more desirable bonds are to be had; people who have invested in this issue want to get their money out for other investments, and it will be a long time before the bond will be redeemed at par.

Yet the fact that a bond or debenture is selling for $10 or even $20 a hundred under par doesn't mean it isn't a good security.

It may be quite a buy for some people. On the other hand, bonds selling for over par, say $105, may be a very bad buy for anyone in very high tax brackets; the yield after taxes may be inconsequential.

A glance at the bond tables in the papers shows that, on June 15, 1963, industrial corporate bonds on the New York Stock Exchange had an average price in the Dow-Jones index of $94.04 per $100 of face value and had dropped 16 cents in 1963. The lowest average for these same bonds in the previous two years was $91.08. Utility bonds in the same averages on the same day were $88.63, down 3 cents on the year—but they had fluctuated more, hitting a low $79.61 in 1961 and a high of $90.20 earlier in 1962.

Railway bonds in the Dow-Jones index had average prices of $84 to $90.

Sprinkled through the Stock Exchange bond list you could find bonds here and there that had shrunk to $40 or even $20, mostly of railroads known to be in trouble. You could also find convertible debentures, identified by the letters "cv," with prices well over $200 or even $300 for $100 of par value. That meant the debentures ultimately could be used to buy common stock in the companies that issued them at bargain prices.

As the long-term bond gets older, and the time nears when it will be redeemed at par or replaced by a new bond, its price generally goes up because it now has ceased to be a long-term bond.

Some bonds have an absolute cash redemption right to the holder at maturity; others the company can replace with new bonds at maturity or even before maturity if it wishes so long as there has been no default. When replacing a bond or debenture issue that is desirable to the investor, with an issue at lower interest rates because the money market has gone down, the company may have to redeem the old bond in new bonds at a bonus, above par. It may also have to pay a bonus over par to retire before maturity, for cash, a debenture issue that has become too expensive in relation to the existing money market.

One kind of bond overlooked by investors is the church bond. Church bonds often are not tax exempt, but they have a remarkably high safety record and the yields from them are better than from federal government bonds or tax exempts, and compare favorably with those of good corporate bonds. A few bond houses specialize in these securities which are issued by Protestant, Catholic and Jewish religious organizations.

I said, a little while back, that *tax exempts don't yield much income*. There are *occasional exceptions*. A Midwest state university recently advertised in a New York paper a small issue priced to yield 5¼ per cent. The advertisement pointed out that, to anyone in the 50 per cent federal tax bracket, this is equivalent to 10½ per cent on the investment.

Most estate planners and investment counselors urge mixing bonds, stocks, insurance and other assets for safety. It all goes back to the childhood adage: "Don't carry all your eggs in one basket." For, in time of rapid inflation, bonds and debentures, except convertible debentures, can be very slow investments; inflation and taxes eat up their income yield, and the principal doesn't grow with rising prices. In fact, it shrinks—because many people don't want to buy bonds then. Yet, even in such times, the bond business goes on, new bonds come out constantly to refinance old bond issues or to help finance national or local government or industrial expansion and operation.

So bonds must be a good thing. But to buy them intelligently requires expert advice.

So, bear in mind . . .

The bond market is no place for the naive.

If you try this field for investment, study the many types of bonds carefully: bonds, debentures, convertible bonds, tax exempts, and so on. Each has its benefits and shortcomings.

Foreign bonds can be dangerous.

There are special situations in bonds, as in stocks, but it is not easy for the amateur to find them.

Beware of hidden clauses in your bonds. Each bond is a contract unto itself.

Tax exempt bonds offer little income, generally. But, there are exceptions to this.

Church bonds are secure but not always tax free.

19. The Amateur Landlord Delusion

Sooner or later, one out of every two homeowners gets the itch to be a landlord.

Perhaps he hears of someone who has a two-family house and gets enough rent for the upstairs apartment to live "practically rent-free." Or, the wife reads some of those advertisements of suburban builders putting up two-family houses, ads that also hold out the lure of an utterly painless mortgage.

The figures sound wonderful and you really can live very cheaply in most two-family houses *so long as you have a good tenant in the second apartment.* But the two-family house is not an ideal real estate investment for several reasons, and having a tenant in your house entails all sorts of risks.

In the first place, the well-designed two-family house is a relatively bigger investment, as a rule, than a one-family house would be. *It is harder to sell* if you get transferred or get into financial difficulties for, in spite of the income feature it offers, the two-family house doesn't appeal to a large number of people.

The apartments in two-family houses are excellent for small families that like to live quietly, don't entertain much and aren't in the habit of acquiring more and more personal belongings. But if there are more than two children, if you like having relatives or friends stay the night, either apartment soon seems horribly cramped.

It's hard to do anything about a two-family house. They nearly always are built on small lots and the necessity of separate main entrances, two kitchens and complete duality leaves no space and no avenue of approach for adding a bedroom, a rumpus room or a carport for an extra car.

It is not always easy to replace a good tenant when you lose one—and sooner or later the tenants move on. It might take two or three months to get another satisfactory tenant. The loss of three months' rent from the second apartment puts a serious hole in your income.

It's easy to get a bad tenant—one who is constantly delinquent in the rent, an arthritic or some other invalid who requires excessive heating in winter (this can run up your fuel bill for the year by as much as $150), or an irresponsible alcoholic or other undesirable. You may be plagued with wild parties and brawling, damage to the walls, floors, plumbing and lighting fixtures, and even by the frequent arrival of a police squad car called by the neighbors.

Such tenants are not as easy to get rid of as you might imagine. So long as they pay the rent, don't set the place on fire or assault you or some member of your family, they can stay until the lease expires—and for many months longer by going into court and swearing (falsely as it may be) that they cannot find another suitable place to live.

Moreover, as an amateur landlord, you are subject to the same *risk of lawsuits by tenants* as the well-financed professional real estate company. If someone in your tenant's family or one of his guests is injured by falling down the stairs (even when drunk) or if, by mischance, your heating system breaks down and someone in the tenant's family becomes quite ill as a result, you might be sued for several times the value of your house. Candidly, these are remote possibilities, but there is some element of this kind of legal risk in renting out living quarters.

Suppose your family grows until you just have to get out of the cramped downstairs apartment, but your real estate man can't find a buyer for your two-family house. He—or you—quickly comes up with the bright idea of renting out both apartments. That will bring in enough income so you can rent a larger apartment or perhaps buy a one-family house to live in (if you happen to have the cash for the down payment). You have virtually no chance of talking the real estate man into taking your equity in the two-family house as a down payment on the one-family house. That probably won't even occur to you; you still are dazzled by the idea of "living rent free" and have no intention of giving up the income from the two-family house and paying all the mortgage costs, taxes and so forth of the new house out of your paycheck.

So the real estate man finds a tenant for your downstairs apartment (or you find the tenant yourself) and gets you a place to live. All goes well at first. On paper, the net income from the old house is a fat 20 per cent a year or more on the money you have in it so far. It's a bigger percentage if you add to profit the amount by which you are amortizing the mortgage. And since you now can depreciate the whole house for tax purposes, all the income from the house likely will be tax free.

Even after you deduct the rent or carrying charges of your new home from the net income (plus tax savings) of the now completely rented two-family house, you may be spending a few dollars less a month and getting better living quarters than you had before.

But you still are an *amateur landlord—and it's almost dead certain that you are living in a fool's paradise.*

The awakening can come about in several ways. Perhaps you lose one tenant and discover he has damaged the apartment shockingly. The cost of repairs plus lost rent is harder to bear than when you lived in the house because you now have the full expense of your new house to carry.

Perhaps you will lose both your tenants almost at once.

You are right on the griddle immediately—two sets of mortgage costs, taxes and other basic expenses to meet out of your paycheck, plus the cost of redecorating two apartments. It is simply impossible to rent an apartment profitably on lease without redecorating it.

Perhaps you don't lose both your tenants, but taxes take a whopping jump in the community because of some improvement, yet you can't raise your rents; your profit margin is cut sharply. Perhaps a big plant in the community closes and your tenants are laid off; like other landlords in the community, much better financed than you are, public opinion will expect you to carry the tenants for a while, perhaps for months. You are in trouble at once. It will do you no good to evict under such circumstances; new tenants simply won't be available.

By this time, you will have begun to suspect what you should have realized from the start—that renting out houses or apartments is much too risky a business for the amateur. Like any other business, it depends on volume and good management, full time management. It takes the net income from a considerable number of units to provide reserves for the many contingent risks, and it takes a lot of time and knowledge to keep the properties in shape and to keep them occupied by reasonably satisfactory tenants.

So the amateur landlord is suffering from a delusion most of the time. Here are some of the reasons why he is deluded—

He does not realize that, as his equity in the property increases, it yields him an ever smaller return on his investment. That's because modern mortgages are level-payment affairs and taxes and other costs remain fairly stationary over the long haul, even though big expenses seem to crop up remarkably suddenly to the inexperienced amateur landlord.

If you have only a $4,000 equity in a house and have

it rented on a basis that brings in $720 a year over and above carrying charges and also amortizes your mortgage by $300 a year, you have a whopping indicated current yield of 25.2 per cent a year from the property.

But, take an identical house after the mortgage has been paid down a number of years and the owner's equity is $15,000. It also brings in $720 over and above carrying charges and the level-payment mortgage now is being amortized at $600 a year—but the indicated yield on the $15,000 the owner has in the house is only 8.8 per cent!

But isn't almost 9 per cent still an excellent yield on an investment?

It would be marvelous on many kinds of securities, but a professional real estate operator would shudder at a 9 per cent indicated yield on such a hazardous and hard-used property as a rental dwelling house. For a topnotch *office building,* a much lower yield might be considered fabulous.

Of course, a real estate agent would collect the rent and otherwise look after the house for the owner—but he certainly wouldn't think of trying to sell such a property to a professional operator.

Remember, the amateur landlord who owns the house that is bringing in 8.8 per cent on his $15,000 equity has all the risks and headaches we mentioned earlier in connection with two-family houses.

These risks make his 8.8 per cent look rather puny even in comparison with the 4 per cent compounded quarterly or semi-annually (with absolutely no risks or headaches) paid by many federal savings and loan associations and savings banks on deposits. It doesn't look as good as the $4\frac{1}{3}$ to $5\frac{1}{2}$ per cent yield you get (at some risk) from good industrial bonds and debentures. It's hardly any better than the yield from some tax-exempt state and municipal bonds which usually are very safe.

The truth is, the amateur landlord with such a big

equity in his house would be better off if he sold, even if he didn't get the full $15,000 for his equity. Then he could put half of the proceeds in bonds or a savings account and the other half in good growth stocks to be held for years—the kind in which $6,000 or $7,000 has a good chance of growing to $25,000 in ten years; should you happen to hit a jackpot such as International Business Machines or some of the better life insurance company stocks have turned out to be in recent years, the $6,000 investment could run up to $100,000.

Finally, the amateur landlord may be deluding himself because of a certain important provision in the federal income tax law. The law says that if you sell the house you live in, and reinvest the proceeds in another house of commensurate value within one year, you need pay no tax on any profit you make on the sale of the old house. You can even buy the new house first, then sell the old house within a year.

But when you sell a house that has been rented out for any length of time, all the profit on the sale is taxable either as straight income or capital gain, depending on the circumstances. Moreover, all the depreciation you have taken off on the house over the years in your income tax returns adjusts the basis in arriving at the taxable gain or loss.

Is it, then, always foolish to rent out a house you own and can't live in?

Not quite. If the house is free and clear—no mortgage —and you can't find a buyer at a price good real estate men tell you it is worth, it certainly pays to rent to a carefully chosen tenant, until such time as the market improves.

If your equity is very small, it may pay to rent the house to a carefully selected tenant until you can accumulate a big enough equity so that a sale will bring you something to reinvest.

Even the chap with the $15,000 equity and the 8.8 per cent yield is better off with his house rented out than standing empty—assuming he has a tenant who will keep the property up—and provided the amateur landlord realizes the dead-end street he is in, and is taking steps to get out.

So, BEAR IN MIND . . .

The amateur landlord is in a position of potential danger, and financial loss.

The most essential element to successful renting is a good tenant.

Most amateur landlords don't appreciate the danger they face from lawsuits by tenants and others.

If you rent out a home you own but don't live in, after a while you lose certain federal tax benefits when you choose to sell the property.

20. True Real Estate Investing

In pointing out the snares the amateur landlord can fall into, I hope I didn't give the impression that real estate isn't a good way to invest savings.

Many people think, with justification, that real estate is the soundest and most profitable of all investments and it can be, when done on a professional basis.

Certainly, over-all land values have gone up as fast or faster than all other values in our national economy during the history of the republic. Great fortunes have been made by land investors and land speculators, and still are being made.

Two of our early presidents, George Washington and Andrew Jackson, were successful land speculators. Washington tramped through the wilderness leading a pack horse carrying his food and his surveyor's instruments. He surveyed the wilderness and sold it off in big tracts at quitclaim rents. (An ancient form of installment sale.) He was much bothered by claim-jumping swindlers who came in behind him and brazenly sold forged deeds to the lands he had surveyed to unwary settlers.

Jackson founded the city of Memphis in partnership with John Overton and James Winchester and also invested and speculated in land in other states, sometimes losing, sometimes making good profits.

Land speculators and developers have played an enormous role in the growth of our country. But not all were successful. Take the chap who bought from Congress for a few cents an acre a huge tract along the Ohio River, some of the most beautiful land in the country. In a year, or so, he went broke, losing around $200,000, a big sum for those days.

But a fellow who bought one lot from this speculator for less than $5 turned around and sold it at a huge profit only a couple of years later. In the late 1950s, a real estate historian traced that lot all the way back and found it was currently appraised at $10.5 million! As you doubtless have guessed, the lot became the heart of downtown Cincinnati.

Robert Morris of Philadelphia was the leading American financier of Colonial days. He largely handled the financing of the Revolution against England. After the war, Morris went into land speculation in a big way. He tried to develop simultaneously enormous tracts in upstate New York, including the present city of Buffalo, and huge tracts near Pittsburgh. The shrewd financier fell into complete disaster and had to be rescued by friends from debtors' prison.

Today, desirable land is becoming scarce in many parts of the United States. That leads to much speculation. The newspapers and the magazines and the mails are filled with the advertising of land developers. Some of the offerings are good, many are not good, and some are outright swindles. Remember: *When you buy land from a speculator you become a speculator, not an investor.*

Excellent profits can be made from good professional real estate investments. They often can pay a *net* return on investment of 8 to 10 per cent a year, some of it tax exempt. They can do this because the yield does not have to come out of taxable profits as in most other business. In real estate investments of a professional nature, the yield comes from "cash flow."

Without being technical about it, net cash flow means actual profit plus the depreciation on the property allowed by the government to offset income taxes. Since the land under the building and the building itself *on the average* will gain in value along with the general economy about as fast as it depreciates for tax purposes, an income may be taken from the depreciation allowance.

This may not be true of a single property, but the professional investor has a number of properties and if one goes sour, he gets rid of it.

How does the small investor get into real estate?

Well, you can buy a building that was put up to yield income and either turn it over to a professional realty man to operate for a commission or devote enough time to the business to learn how to run it professionally. Turning it over to a professional is probably the best way.

A building with four or five apartments, perhaps with a shop on the first floor in a good commercial-residential neighborhood is such an investment, if you take great care in choosing it.

A still better way is to go into a small syndicate partnership with a good real estate operator—but stay out of big real estate syndications that are advertised in the papers. They have been so overdone and so watered-down in recent years that many of them are in serious trouble.

The small syndication works something like this. Realty Operator Jones has his eye on a successful apartment house or a small commercial building that is for sale. Jones needs about $25,000 more than he has on hand to swing the deal, and borrowing it might over-extend him. So he offers to take five people in as partners, each to put up $5,000. A syndicate is formed. Jones has the biggest stake and, since he is putting the deal together and carrying the burden of operating the property after it is bought, he gets the biggest return.

With such sound small syndications, the partners who put up the $5,000 shares (it might be more or even less) often can count on a good steady yield of 7, 8 or even 10 per cent.

The main trouble about such investments is they are hard to sell if you need your money for an emergency.

Lately, a number of public real estate investment companies have been formed that sell shares to the public. The shares pay dividends out of cash flow. A few pay as much as 7 to 7½ per cent return on the price of the stock. The yield to the investor from both syndications and these real estate investment company shares may well be exempt for a long period from federal income tax under the theory that it is return of principal rather than income. Only income and capital gains are taxable under the income tax laws.

However, a lot of real estate investment companies have gotten into difficulties in recent years and great care must be exercised in investing in their securities.

Here are a few tests for a good sound real estate investment company stock:

1. The company should be primarily an investing-operating firm, not a trading company. The cash flow from which dividends are paid should come entirely from rentals and depreciation, not from proceeds or gain on sales of property. The company should promptly reinvest proceeds of sales of property.

2. It should have a policy of owning outright (subject to mortgages) the properties it operates, either by itself or through net leases to managing companies. Speculators can sometimes make money out of leases and subleases, but investors can't.

3. It should be a sound equity outfit—having an average equity of 30 per cent or more in all its properties, not a "leverage" outfit trying to carry and operate a huge portfolio of properties on equities as thin as 10 per cent.

4. If the company engages in building, watch out. Only extremely experienced people can make money out of building under today's conditions.

So, bear in mind . . .

If you choose real estate as your investment, don't buy from a speculator unless you wish to speculate. Investment is something else again.

Additional real estate profits are to be made through the depreciation allowance.

It will pay you to use the services of a professional realty man.

If you can avoid the frauds and promoters, a syndicate partnership with a professional real estate man can be profitable to you.

Check carefully before you buy stock in a real estate investment company. There are good companies in this field—and bad ones.

21. Tax Headaches

So you think paying taxes is rough today!

Consider the way the Pharaohs taxed the peasants in ancient Egypt. If the peasant was a little bit short of what the tax gatherer assessed against him he was flogged and one of his oxen was seized. If he was short more, one of his children was taken to be sold as a slave. If he owed the king a good round sum and couldn't pay, all his children, his wife and his animals might be taken.

If he couldn't pay anything at all, the tax gatherer, annoyed at the loss of his fee, likely as not would have the poor peasant flung into the Nile to feed the crocodiles.

Things were no better in the Babylonian and Persian empires. Even in comparatively enlightened Greece and Rome, people were sold into slavery by the thousands for tax delinquency. Nor were the tax rates in the ancient empires low. They were levied most heavily on the peasants and small landlords and often amounted to one-third or more of the total crop.

England and France were the first countries where the barons became strong enough to limit the taxing power of the monarch and to introduce some humanity into the taxing system, although, insofar as the peasantry was concerned, the tax laws were still pretty harsh down to the 19th Century.

Nor did England's stiff-necked kings learn easily all the harsh realities about the attitude of people toward taxes. Britain lost the most valuable of all of her colonial possessions because one of her kings insisted on enforcing some rather mild taxes on the American colonists which the colonists had not had a share in voting.

You still can go to jail for *cheating* on taxes or *willful refusal* to pay, as folks find out every now and then in this country. Ironically, *the small taxpayer is in greater danger of being convicted if he is accused of willful tax evasion than is the millionaire.* A jury, sworn to consider every possibility of a reasonable doubt, is likely to think it reasonable that a multimillionaire might be telling the truth when he says he forgot about an item of $30,000. But, what jury is going to believe that a family on an income of six or seven thousand a year really forgot to include in its tax return a bonanza of $500?

So, if you want to sleep well nights, make it a rule early in a life that *cheating the tax gatherer is risky.* People always have tried to cheat the tax gatherer, and some have succeeded, but Mortimer Caplin, chief of the Internal Revenue Service, has been rushing around the country making speeches giving fair warning that, from now on, *everybody's* income from nearly all sources is going to be checked by electronic computers. It's sheer foolishness to take the risk of lying in your income tax return.

Professional groups that make their livings by viewing our rising tax rates with alarm keep telling us that we should be "tax conscious" the whole year around—and not just from April 1 to April 15. They are right in their contention, but "conscious" isn't exactly the right word. We're all tax conscious from the time we can read, even before. When Dad stops at the gas station to fill the tank, the kids can read the sign on the pump which tells what a shocking portion of the price of a gallon of fuel is taxes.

In some states, kids learn even before they can read that there's a penny tax on a dime candy bar. And a girl in one of the sales tax states certainly has become tax "conscious" by the time she buys her first lipstick.

Boys and girls often get a social security number when

they are only fourteen and acquire a working knowledge of social security taxes and even income withholding taxes.

So what we need is people who are "tax *concerned*" the whole year—not just tax conscious.

One of the biggest family tax problems is *the disinclination of the wife to make advance provision for taxes.* She doesn't want to hear about taxes. She doesn't want to learn how to make out a family income tax return or, even, to look over the joint return before she signs it. On all questions of what should be declared and what deductions should be taken, her attitude is, take off everything you can think of. The total amount of tax always seems appalling to her, and she is annoyed that her husband isn't clever enough to think of more ways to reduce it. As for the required declaration and payment on estimated income for the coming year, she is inclined to think it a good idea to skip that—"How do we know we'll make that much this year, anyway?"

Often a prudent husband wishes to have the payroll department at his office drop one of his exemptions from the withholding tax so he won't come up at the end of the year owing the government money; this annoys the wife no end, she thinks the government is getting the money too soon. And, sometimes a working wife makes trouble by taking duplicate exemptions from payroll tax on her salary; then she screams when her husband glumly informs her at the end of the year that they owe Uncle Sam a wad because not enough tax has been taken out of her pay.

However, it is not true that all women—or even most women—think taxes are something to pay only when the federal marshal or the sheriff drives up with a warrant. I have gone into this matter to emphasize that every bridegroom ought to insist that his wife become tax concerned. Of course there is a drawback—you can't teach your wife how to make out the tax return without letting her find out how much you make. And I have heard that there still are men so old-fashioned that they don't want the little woman to know how much they make.

The small-time accountant who has a sign in the window saying he makes out income tax returns for five bucks is usually an honest and competent Joe, but his services are not a good investment. Every small taxpayer living primarily on salary *should learn to make out his own return*. Only the man who has a business of his own, or real estate and other investment income, should require the services of a tax accountant. If you are in that class, you need a good honest tax accountant *on a year-round retainer* so you can call him up and discuss the tax angles of any deal you think about going into.

I put in "honest" because I happen to remember the sad case of a big city restaurateur, who worked fourteen hours a day for years to take care of his rapidly growing clientele and couldn't figure out why he was losing money. Then one day, his trusted tax accountant, who handled his money as well as his tax records, went on vacation and the restaurant man had to do some of the tax work himself. In no time, he discovered that his restaurant, instead of losing money, had made more than $100,000 over and above his own salary in the past half-dozen years—but the trusted tax accountant had stolen practically all of it!

The pamphlets the Internal Revenue Service mails out with Form 1040 contain in clear and detailed language enough instructions for most people to make out their own returns, and you can obtain special instruction sheets from the nearest Internal Revenue office on almost any point not covered in the pamphlet.

The big savings to be made on income taxes are on investment income, and on the buying and selling of securities and other property. This is largely a matter of when to do what, and it can be accomplished only with expert advice, as a rule. The person with enough income and property to profit by these tax savings will need the advice of professional consultants.

However, it is probable that *many people still pay more income tax than they should* out of sheer carelessness. They do not trouble to read the instructions carefully and they use the wrong form or the wrong tax table or they fail to file a joint husband-and-wife return, which is cheaper, and is permissible even if the wife had no income during the year.

Others have paid too much taxes by simply making flagrant mistakes in arithmetic. Since the use of automatic machines for checking arithmetic in tax returns began, the IRS has been somewhat astonished to find that taxpayers' cheat themselves by their mistakes in figuring at least as often as they short-change Uncle Sam!

One big source of tax loss for many families is an unfair real estate tax on the home. I certainly don't want to suggest that most or even as much as a third of home assessments are unfair, but, local politics being what they are, there are outrageous inequities in the tax assessment rolls in virtually every community in the United States. When you buy a house, it is a good idea to make an inquiry and find out how your tax bill compares with your neighbor's. The real estate man from whom you buy or the bank from whom you obtain your mortgage may be helpful in this task.

If you conclude that you are unfairly assessed, you have a right of appeal. The procedure for seeking a readjustment varies tremendously in different states. Often the appeal must be filed at a certain period of the year and is heard at a stated meeting of a board of adjustment. It would be naive to suppose that considerable political log-rolling is not involved in local tax assessments. The assessors are trying to raise as much money from the tax rolls as they can and they are under constant pressure from the local big wheels for favored treatment. But remember the old rural adage—"It's the squeaking wheel that gets the grease." If you don't investigate, you won't know if you are being gouged; and if you don't complain if you are, you won't get relief.

Income taxes at once brings up the question of contributions. Be very careful about deducting any amount from your taxable income for contributions that you cannot verify. The IRS is well aware that the privilege of making deductions for contributions has been flagrantly abused in the past and all returns are given a check for the ratio of contributions to total income.

Not only is there now a legal ceiling on the proportion —20 per cent—of your income (and, in some cases, 30 per cent) that may be deducted for contributions, but remember that listing a phony contribution is not just an error in your return, it is an act of fraud and lays you open to criminal charges.

Contributions pay off in tax savings just as they pay off in life. In spite of the new ceiling on the total amount of contributions that can be deducted, it is still possible for the well-to-do to drop their taxable income into a lower rate bracket by making contributions to worthwhile causes. So when you contribute to good causes, from 16 to 77% of the cost for the taxable year beginning in 1964 and from 14 to 77% of the taxable years after 1964 is tax money, depending on how rich you are.

Why does the government allow large deductions for contributions? In obedience to religious and philosophical precepts thousands of years old, tested and proved by time to be absolutely essential to social progress. Our great hospitals, universities and charitable institutions could not have come into being without them and churches live on contributions.

We all know that the chap who refuses when the hat is passed at the office (for a gift for the stenographer who is getting married) is looked on as a louse; so is the guy who doesn't give to the Community Fund, the volunteer fire company or the hospital's annual drive in his town.

All great religious leaders have said contributions earned a great reward. Jesus said: "Cast thy bread upon the waters and it shall be returned thee many fold."

Interest paid on money borrowed is deductible for tax purposes. As a matter of fact, it has become quite unfashionable, particularly for one with a large income, not to have taken advantage of this deductible feature in the tax law.

Interest paid on your mortgage, your car, your instalment purchases, are all deductible in arriving at your taxable income. Interest paid on loans secured by stocks or bonds are also deductible.

Medical expenses should be watched, since the tax law affords deductions under varying circumstances.

A surprising number of people don't think about *estate taxes* on what property they will leave, until too late.

Yet within fifteen months after the last tears are shed for you, Uncle Sam's tax agents may come knocking at the door asking your wife for a substantial estate tax— not just on what you left her but on everything you owned at the time of your death, providing you owned property worth $120,000, and you qualify for the maximum marital deduction, otherwise on property worth $60,000.

The heirs of a bachelor or bachelor girl can be taxed by Uncle Sam on an estate of only $60,000. Most of the states also have estate taxes, but they generally are small and are usually deductible from the federal tax.

The federal estate tax starts at 3 per cent and runs up to 77 per cent for the very rich. It is not worthwhile in this book to go into a detailed discussion of estate taxes, but it is necessary to advise people who begin in middle life to acquire a little property to think about estate tax problems and to start consulting their bankers and financial advisers so that they can tailor every important business step they take in life so as to hold their ultimate tax obligation to a minimum.

So, bear in mind . . .

If you keep tax-conscious all year round, there will be no panic or financial trouble when payment time arrives.

Your wife may find it difficult (as many wives do) to make advance provision for taxes. Work with her on this.

If you and your wife both work, make sure that you are not taking duplicate exemptions. Eventually, you must pay up!

Learn how to make out your own return—unless your financial activities in investments require a professional. Then, retain an accountant on a year-round basis.

Many people pay more tax than they should because they have not spent sufficient time studying this field.

Check to see if your house is overappraised for tax purposes. If it is, do something about it. If you don't help yourself, who will?

Prepare now to keep the taxes on your estate as low as possible. Your survivors will suffer if you are careless.

22. Financing Education

Parents worry far more today than in the past about the cost of educating children. They generally are convinced that, in today's world, the boy without a college degree hasn't a chance and the girl without a college social background is unlikely to make a good marriage.

To some extent these fears are justified. With more than 2,000 universities and colleges in the land, it is estimated that the undergraduate campus population in the 1963-64 academic year will be 4.2 million. That is a high percentage of the boys and girls between 17 and 22; so, on numbers alone, it is clear that the adolescent who does not go to college will be at a competitive disadvantage.

Forty years ago, or even during the Great Depression, a lad could start as a clerk or a salesman with a big company and work himself up on sheer merit and industry with little regard to formal education. That is demonstrably impossible today in most big companies. They will not accept an application from a boy for an office or sales job unless he has a college degree. Moreover, big companies nearly all have definite executive training programs for which they recruit youngsters fresh from college on the basis of grades, aptitude tests, social background and other factors.

In the office or factory of any big corporation today you can find numerous situations like this:

Jim D. and Jack J. work at adjoining desks in the design department of Space Age Industries, Inc., which, in spite of its name, makes rather prosaic electrical components.

Jim and Jack do identical work and draw the same pay. If anything, Jim is a bit the more industrious of the two, is quite as intelligent as Jack and to impartial eyes, even seems a trifle more personable. But Jim isn't going anyplace with Space Age Industries—and sooner or later he will realize it. Jack, on the other hand, is destined to move up in the company even though he is not kin to any major stockholder and never has met the president of the company.

Jack was hired as part of the company's executive training program through a firm of professional recruiters. He is from a prestige college where he had a 90-plus average and made the varsity basketball team, he comes of a family with good social background, and he made high scores on aptitude and general interest tests.

The company will move Jack up and around on a definite schedule during the next few years and may even send him to university and institutional management seminars to prepare him for steady promotion. All Jack has to do to get ahead is keep his nose clean and do as he's told.

Jim, on the other hand, was hired just to do his present job; no matter how well he does it, the company has no special interest in him and no incentive to set aside its investment in Jack to give Jim a chance to advance. Only a miracle can enable Jim to get anywhere in Space Age Industries—and Jim has a college education.

Undemocratic? Maybe. But who is naive enough to imagine that any industrial corporation is a pure democracy?

This kind of roadblock lies ahead in virtually all industries for the millions of young Americans who are wasting their adolescent years "goofing off." A vast number of them won't get into college at all and, with automated technology wiping out unskilled industrial and commercial jobs by the millions, this nation faces an extremely difficult task in the next generation in managing to find a way for these young men to earn their keep. There is little question but that, for the next generation at least, technological unemployment and hard core unemployment of people who are intellectually or emotionally incapable of earning a living, are both going to increase.

Nevertheless, I think parents worry too much about getting their children into college. *Not all youngsters are college material.* Some boys are ready at seventeen—the freshman age—to come to grips with life in commerce or industry and simply lack the incentive or temperament to spend four years learning by book. Remember, theory without practice seldom works.

And, there are still plenty of businesses and careers for men without college training although, it must be confessed, they all lie outside the big corporations. The non-college man certainly will do better going into business for himself early in life.

Nor does either a boy or a girl need a college degree to have good social standing and make a good marriage. Today's young people are much more sensible than that about picking life partners.

Finally, don't take it too seriously if your youngster doesn't make a high score on the aptitude test often used by both colleges and industry. The high score in an aptitude test usually is meaningful, but the low score isn't, with teen-agers. A low score may merely mean the youngster isn't quite ready. The experience of many companies in employing young people who have made either high or low scores on aptitude tests confirms this. The aptitude test is an unreliable criterion at best and certainly no panacea.

The young man who does not manage to get to college may make a better living and get ahead faster than the lad with the high I.Q. and good background who is eagerly hunted by the recruiters of corporation executive trainees.

But, he will have to be capable of tremendous self-discipline and self-improvement. He will have to be able to make himself work six days a week for ten to fourteen hours a day while others put in a forty-hour week. He will have to spend his evenings in study instead of at the ballpark, or slumped in front of the TV set with a can of beer, or out with the fellows looking for girls.

That not only takes character, it takes sacrifice—and most parents rightly don't want to gamble on their children being able to do it. Particularly fathers who succeeded in doing it themselves want to make certain their sons don't have to do it—but get to a good college and have an even break with more fortunate children.

So the parents want to know how to save enough money to be sure tuition bills can be met if Junior makes good enough grades in high school to get into college.

At the risk of sounding like the rankest of heretics, my advice is—don't.

Don't set up a specific saving program for college tuition, that is.

I admit this advice would have been quite wrong in past eras, but I am sure it is right for the present for three reasons:

1. The cost of a college education has gone up so rapidly in recent years that it defeats special tuition savings programs.

2. The number of tuition-free community junior colleges is increasing rapidly. The knowledge that, if they want to go to college, they must try to win entrance to one of these institutions first can be a great incentive to youngsters to work hard in high school.

3. The early marriage vogue of the years since World War II has meant that couples have been in such a rush to get married and have babies that the older children fre-

quently reach college age before the father is forty years old. That means Pop may not have reached the peak of his earning power. In fact, it may be much easier for him to pay the costs of sending his children to college while they are there and after they have graduated than to save up for it in advance.

Just as putting too much money in too big a house or too big an automobile may leave the family without capital to take advantage of excellent investment opportunities, so a commitment to a savings fund specifically for college tuition may not only be a monthly hardship, but it also can cause the father to pass up investment opportunities that would in time reap enough earnings and capital growth to do far more for the family than just educate the children.

The first reason alone should suffice to show the present impracticality of specific savings programs for college tuition for most people. Let's demonstrate. Some years ago it was a popular idea for a young man about twenty-one to buy a twenty-year endowment life insurance policy, often in a mutual company, for a face amount of $2,000. The idea was that it would mature about the time his oldest son was ready for college, and, in those days, you really could put a boy through a state university and many good smaller private colleges for a little more than $2,000.

Today, the minimum cost of a college education, except in the community junior colleges, is around $7,000. At Harvard, Lehigh, M.I.T. and other such prestige institutions, it's around $12,000. A complete medical education comes closer to $30,000. The premiums on enough endowment life insurance to pay these costs would be too high, and we have already seen in the chapter on life insurance that, under today's conditions, endowment insurance is neither good protection nor a cheap way to save.

How, then, are college expenses to be financed?

I think in two main ways—by loans and by the earnings of the boys and girls themselves, plus whatever Pop can spare from his regular budget. Since custom, the law and parental inclination dictate that boys and girls are entitled to be fed, clothed, sheltered and doctored at family expense until approximately the end of their college days—Pop ought to be prepared to pay these items right out of his paycheck while the kids are away on campus, just as when they are at home.

That leaves tuition, books, laboratory fees, laundry, spending money, etc., to be paid for by loans and what the youngsters can earn during summer months and in part-time jobs during the school year.

Virtually all colleges try to help students find part-time work and employ placement experts to do so. However, many colleges are in communities where part-time job opportunities are scarce.

About forty years ago the University of Cincinnati and Antioch College at Yellow Springs, Ohio, worked out what they called the co-operative plan to attack this problem. The student is offered a work-study program under which he spends alternating periods of several weeks each studying on the campus and working full time on a job.

At Antioch, the entire student body was put on this co-op plan, with pairs of students covering a full-time job in a factory or office perhaps several hundred miles from the campus. The plan is still in effect and has been a huge success.

Variations on this work-study program have been adopted at many other universities and colleges according to local conditions, although I have not heard of any others on the scale of Antioch's. The only objection to the Antioch plan is that it stretches out the conventional four-year undergraduate course to five years.

Some professional colleges have very good work-study programs. The College of Insurance of New York provides its students with a practical work-study program for insurance companies or organizations while they are doing classroom work leading to a degree.

The earning capacity of college boys and girls fluctuates considerably from year to year. The kids who went to college in the late 1940s and early 1950s had it lucky. Part-time jobs were plentiful on many campuses and so were summer jobs. It was not at all unusual for students, especially girls who were good at secretarial work, to have little trouble earning more than 40 per cent of their college expenses in those days. That meant Pop had to carry only a small note at the bank, renewed each semester, to keep things in even keel.

Presently, campus part-time jobs are not plentiful and summer jobs are hard to get, college placement bureaus report, while the big rise in college costs has taken place in the past eight years. So the kids can't earn as much, on the average. Boys in advanced science, engineering and pre-medical courses have virtually no time to devote to earning money, anyway; the academic load in these fields is too heavy—two to three times as heavy as in the 1930s.

So Pop has to borrow somewhat more heavily to keep the youngsters in college than was the case ten years ago. Fortunately commercial banks, finance companies and some other lending institutions saw this trend developing and nudged by college presidents, began setting up loan plans to meet it. At first, the lending institutions considered this as primarily public service business designed mainly to build goodwill. But very soon they found that making tuition loans could be an extremely profitable business even at relatively modest interest rates and fees. So more and more banks and finance companies have gone into the business.

In fact, the time may not be far off when the problem of financing a college education for your children requires only a little more foresight and sacrifices than the problem of buying a rather big automobile.

But you can save an awful lot by getting your youngsters into a tuition-free community college for the freshman and sophomore years.

And if your youngsters have touches of genius, they may win scholarships. Some scholarships are available on the basis of need too, rather than special ability.

And then there's the outside chance that Junior is a sure-fire future all-America quarterback or a six-foot-seven sure-shot on the maple floor. He's got it made. Your problem is to keep him from getting a big head.

SO, BEAR IN MIND . . .

The simple truth is, not all children are college material. Some children may do better for themselves if they enter business earlier, without passing time at school which cannot benefit them.

There is no point to saving for a child's future college education. This money is best invested along with your other investment funds.

Student loans, part-time jobs, and bank tuition loans are available when the need arises.

The twenty-year endowment life insurance policy method of saving for college expenses is unwise, expensive and outdated.

23. Wills and Widows

One of the fundamental facts of life that many people just don't face is that, nowadays, *most women eventually become widows.* Not only is the wife usually a year or more younger than her spouse but the great advances in obstetrics and gynecology have given women a definite edge over men in longevity.

Yet an enormous number of women, many of them quite intelligent and well educated, become widows every year with virtually no preparation for such a drastic economic change.

Wives and husbands have the queerest illusions about this problem. Often they imagine that a life insurance policy of $10,000 or $20,000 will tide the widow over until she can start earning a substantial sum. They forget that funeral expenses, perhaps piled on top of big hospital and medical bills growing out of the husband's last illness, make a big dent in the insurance proceeds. And how about the indebtedness on ordinary charge accounts and installment accounts that now suddenly must be met and settled without the husband's husky monthly paycheck?

I have pointed out earlier the reluctance of many women to think about the possibility, indeed the strong likelihood, of widowhood. They don't want to talk about life insurance; they don't want to learn how to make an income tax return. They are not eager to learn anything about investments.

Working wives are less prone to this neurotic attitude than the stay-at-home housewife.

But husbands are just as shortsighted. Very few men under sixty actually stop and figure out what their wives would have to live on if they were to be killed in an auto accident tomorrow. Even the chap who has bought life insurance on a well-planned program would have a difficult time explaining exactly what Janie and the kids should do with the insurance money if he were to die tomorrow.

Some married women who had good jobs when they were single cling to the comforting illusion that they could get just as good jobs quickly if they were widowed. But many a widow in her late thirties or early forties finds her services are not particularly in demand; she is horrified at being offered hardly enough to meet the monthly mortgage payment she and her husband have been making.

Moreover, if there still are young children, day nursery costs will eat heavily into whatever pay the widow can make as a secretary, teacher or saleswoman.

The truth is that it is more important for comparatively young couples to make some preparation against the possible death of either husband or wife than for older persons. When an elderly woman is widowed, her children probably are grown and able and willing to help her and the number of years she must be cared for or take care of herself may not be too many.

But if a woman of thirty with two small children suddenly loses her husband, she faces a long, hard struggle, often with no one to whom she has a natural right to turn for help.

Young couples usually do not understand that they also should make some preparations against the risk of the wife's sudden death. For example, many young couples keep the checking account in the wife's name because she has to pay most of the bills anyway. They also put the house and the savings account in the wife's name. Someone has told them they will save inheritance taxes in case Bill dies suddenly. Also, during one period when the wolf in the person of a tribe of bill collectors was storming the door it seemed a good idea to put things in Susie's name where they couldn't be attached legally.

But suppose Susie dies suddenly and there has been no preparation for this in the shape of a will. Bill suddenly finds the checking account and the savings account are tied up by the bank officer whose duty it is to read the obituaries in the newspapers.

Under the law of most states, Bill inherits only one-third of the bank accounts and the house that are in Susie's name; the other two-thirds goes to the children, and until the children are grown, Bill can't do anything with their property without permission of the court! In order to straighten out the snarl, he must hire a lawyer and pay him a rather substantial fee.

If there are no children, the situation can be worse. Bill's in-laws can claim half of his bank accounts and hold the house as joint heirs with him to Susie's estate.

If a man who has been separated for years from a wife who deserted him but from whom he has not been finally divorced, dies without leaving a will, she can claim a third of his estate if there are children, half of it if there are no children.

These hazards are mitigated in some states by exemptions that give a childless spouse all of an estate of less than $10,000 when there is no will.

Not having a properly drawn will can subject even a modest estate to many hazards and to extra taxation. If there is a will and the house and the balance of the estate are willed to the surviving spouses, taxes generally are lower than if the estate is divided according to the statute for those who die without a will.

As we have seen by the case of Bill and Susie, it is vitally necessary for the wife to make a will if any major part of the family possessions are in her name. But even

if nothing is in her name, there is another vitally important reason why she should make a will.

Nowadays, many couples die together in automobile
or aircraft accidents, or they may die from natural causes
within a short time of each other.

In such cases, if the wife has no will and the authorities decide that she survived her husband, even if only
by one minute, then she became the possessor of whatever
part of the estate her husband's will left her—and that
part of the estate is up for grabs among her heirs, since
she has died intestate.

All of these harrowing possibilities can be averted by
spending a modest fee *to hire a competent lawyer to draw
wills for both husband and wife.*

You should be in a hurry to decide to make a will,
but you should take a little time to think about how you
really want to dispose of your property. Above all, do not
withhold any information from the lawyer you engage.
He can't provide for contingencies if you don't tell him
about the legal strings tied to your property under the
will of Aunt Emma, who left it to you, for example. And
he should be told of any possibility that relatives you dis-
like might attack your will in court so he can set up
defense against the attack.

In most states, only one copy of a will can be signed.
The existence of a second signed copy invalidates the will.

Generally a will must be witnessed by two persons,
neither of whom is an heir under it or is closely related
to the testor. A will should name an executor and an administrator. A good plan for a small estate is to name your
spouse as first choice and someone younger and competent, a trusted lawyer, bank official or very close relative,
as joint or alternate executor.

One of the most important reasons for having a will
is to make sure you can name the executor of the will
and the administrator for the property. If there is no

will, there is no certainty that the court will appoint your wife (or your husband) to execute the will and administer the property. A stranger might be named to look after your property and may even be appointed legal guardian of your children.

Without wanting to be an alarmist, I have to point out that in comparatively recent years, several rings of dishonest probate judges and unscrupulous lawyers have been uncovered in the United States; these were vultures who made a practice of looting the estates of well-to-do people who died intestate by obtaining the appointment of court favorites as administrators of the estates, then selling off all the assets at ridiculous prices to dummy buyers representing the crooked judge and lawyers. They left the widows and orphans virtually penniless!

The naming of a guardian for your children if your wife should predecease you or if you should both die in an accident is important. Otherwise there might be an unpleasant fight over the children and the court might give their custody to the relative you and your wife might least desire to bring them up.

There are sharp statutory limits on what you can do with your property in your will. In only two states, the Dakotas, can a man disinherit his wife or a wife disinherit her husband outrightly (provided they have not been legally divorced). In other states, a wife or husband may be excluded from inheriting either real estate or personal property but in most states it is difficult or impossible to deprive her or him of at least one-third of the estate. Also in most states a certain minimum share of the estate may not be disposed of at all by will but passes automatically to the wife or husband and children. In New York, this provision covers $1,000 in cash, one automobile, farm animals and implements, a sixty-day supply of groceries and the family Bible. This property also is exempt from estate taxes as a rule.

As we have pointed out before proceeds of a life insurance policy cannot be willed unless the policy is payable to one's estate. Neither can U.S. Treasury Savings Bonds be willed if they are made payable to an individual beneficiary in case of death.

Your will must be kept safely. An insurance company normally will pay off if the policy has been mislaid years ago if you have paid the premiums. But a court demands the production of the original will or very strong proof of its existence and that it has not been revoked. Such proof is not easy to produce. Contrary to what you may have read in fiction, *holographic wills* (all in your own handwriting and not properly witnessed) and oral wills made in the presence of witnesses, *are not readily accepted at law* and may be rejected altogether. A safety deposit box is a good place to keep your will—and your wife's.

In some states, the moment one spouse dies and the bank hears about it, half of the joint checking and joint savings account is frozen. Nor will a bank honor a check signed by a man who has died, as a rule. Court records are full of cases where checks that were actually presented before the death of the signer at the payee's bank have been rejected by the signer's bank because he died while the check was in transit—even though there was money in the account to cover the check.

Safe deposit boxes also are sealed by banks, even if they are in the name of both husband and wife, on the death of one partner (in some states) until the tax appraiser arrives.

The point of all this is that younger women need to get over their morbid dread of widowhood and face the fact that it is a strong possibility and *they must be prepared for it.*

Surprisingly, many of us do not think about Social Security insurance for widows and surviving children or even realize they are entitled to it until directly faced with the problem. We think of Social Security solely as old age insurance; actually it is also life insurance and sometimes pays off quite handsomely as life insurance.

Consider Tom T., a mechanic who died in 1959 at the age of 33, leaving a wife and three children. For Social Security purposes, Tom's average monthly wage figured out at $300. This entitled his widow and children immediately to $236.40 a month until the oldest child becomes 18, the amount to be diminished thereafter as the other children reach 18. However, if Tom's widow elected to work, she could collect Social Security only for the children, not for herself, until she reached retirement age. But for many widows with three young children, $236.40 a month is a substantial sum on top of whatever other resources they have. The flaw in this is that the maximum monthly allowance for either old age insurance or survivor's insurance under Social Security is $254.10 and you have to be fully insured; that is, you must have worked the full minimum number of required quarters and must have averaged around $400 a month in pay since 1950, and you must have dependent children, in order to get that much. And $254.10 a month is not enough for a widow to live on and raise children in most parts of this country. So Social Security benefits only mitigate the hardships of most widows. Social Security cannot make them comfortable.

So, bear in mind . . .

Most women eventually become widows. You must face up to this problem and prepare for it.

A widow depends heavily on the funds left to her. It is almost impossible for her to return to work, and social security payments are inadequate.

You should also consider, and prepare for, the possibility that wife will pre-decease husband. Bank accounts in her name will be sealed at her death and needed funds will be withheld from the husband.

The husband and wife should *each* make a will, *now*. Have a skilled lawyer do this for you. Greedy in-laws and time delays are typical of the hazards of dying intestate. Also, now, name a guardian for your children should both parents die.

Safe deposit boxes, held by both spouses together, will be sealed by the bank if one dies.

Your wills must be kept in a safe place, immediately available when they are required. Ask your lawyer about this problem.

24. Retirement and Pensions

Of all the evils of modern American society, certainly one of the most cruel is forced retirement at age 65.

A policeman, a fireman, an airline pilot, a soldier, or a sailor must retire in the early sixties and many of them quit much earlier voluntarily because their livelihoods are dangerous and depend on being physically rugged. Governments and airlines have recognized this and the pensions of these men are accordingly more liberal.

But *compulsory retirement of executives, professional men and office and craft workers*—just when a majority are at the peak of their intellectual powers and usefulness —*is a criminal waste and cruelly oppressive.*

I concede the right and duty of any company to replace an executive or professional who has lost his drive and "no longer has it." But that can happen to a man in his early forties as readily as in his early sixties; the decision to get rid of the executive or professional who has slowed down alarmingly or to put him on the shelf in a less responsible and less arduous job should be faced up to by responsible management on an individual basis. Responsibility should not be evaded by hiding behind a blanket policy of retiring everybody at 65, the brilliant and vigorous along with the mediocre and the minority who actually are way over the hill.

Where does the pressure for compulsory retirement in industry, commerce and the professions come from anyway? It doesn't come from the older men themselves. Those who want to retire will do so voluntarily at the earliest possible moment instead of waiting for the mandatory retirement age. Nor does the pressure come from the creative and vigorous minds in an enterprise; these usually are keenly aware of the loss occasioned by the compulsory retirement of able men at the height of their powers.

Rather, the pressure comes from the mediocrities of society, men who have little ability and no hope of distinction, authority or rewards except to inherit them through default, by the sterile march of seniority aided now and then by a bit of sordid backbiting and cunning office politics.

In the trade unions, there is pressure for compulsory retirement from the apprentices and two-thirders and from journeymen with younger brothers and sons they want to get into the union. But here again, the real issue is not faced.

That issue is: *When is a man old?*

Is he old because he has lived 65 years? Maybe, but just maybe.

We are more logical about machines than we are about ourselves. We measure the age of an automobile, a tire, or a machine in a factory not merely by the number of years since it was made, but by the amount of use it has been put to, by the amount of wear its various parts show when tested and by whether a better machine has been invented or designed for the same purpose since it was bought.

In that way we accept the fact that one machine may be ready for retirement when it is less than two years old and another may be still extremely useful when it is past thirty years old. But we arbitrarily decide that all men and women are worn out when they are sixty-five, certainly no later than that and no sooner unless they just collapse and won't run any longer.

In terms of coming to grips with the needs of society

and industry some people are as "old" as they ever will be when they are eighteen. They have ceased to be able to absorb education since about the sixth grade in school, and show neither a capacity nor inclination to learn further about living and getting along in the world. The only quality about many of these youngsters likely to increase is their capacity for getting in trouble and involving other people in their misfortunes.

Theodore Roosevelt was regarded as a great humanitarian, but Teddy had his moments of severe disillusionment with the great unwashed who voted him into office. While he was President he told his friend Owen Wister, the novelist who wrote *The Virginian,* that he could cheerfully wish that 70 per cent of the American people would just disappear because they were vulgar, stupid, useless to themselves and generally offensive to decent and intelligent people. Wister was discreet enough not to publish this until after Teddy was dead.

Things haven't changed since TR's time; indeed they may have gotten worse. Just a few years ago, a scientist on the staff of the Rockefeller Foundation in New York made a speech that stunned a huge national parent-teacher gathering in Chicago. He said the medical profession had on its conscience the preserving alive of a horde of hulking moronic boys and girls and adults who would have died of childhood diseases in former times. The scientist, a medical man, implied pretty strongly that he thought it might be still better to let a large proportion of our children die early because they are weaklings and misfits who never will be anything but burdens to their parents and society.

The Chicago audience included a lot of do-gooder educators, psychologists, social workers and clergymen. Naturally, the doctor's tough philosophy shocked the pants off many of them. By the time the doctor got back to New York, the roof was about to fall in on him. He clammed up and refused to talk with newspaper and magazine reporters eager to follow up his speech.

As they reach their middle thirties, those people who have wasted their younger years and accomplished nothing cast hungry eyes at the seniority-fattened paychecks of the older workers and they press at union meetings and elsewhere for ever-earlier forced retirement. In a more ruthless society, such as the beehive, drones are liquidated when they have completed their usefulness.

Retirement inevitably means a big reduction in income and standard of living to all except the extremely successful. If this reduction is accepted voluntarily, it is not humiliating. But when it is forced on a man and his wife, just at the time when they feel they are accomplishing more than they ever have before, it is not only humiliating and frustrating, it is downrightly degrading and unjust.

In addition, *compulsory retirement increases the cost of Social Security* and of all private pension programs. Most people do not realize how much Social Security already costs—3⅝ per cent of gross payrolls up to $4,800 per worker levied on both worker and employee up to 1968—a total of 7¼ per cent of all industrial, commercial and professional payrolls up to $4,800 a year per worker. After 1968, the rate will rise gradually to 5⅝ per cent against both worker and employer. That is a very substantial insurance premium.

If fewer workers were compelled to retire at 65 and claim their benefits, the prospect of this rate continuing to rise in the coming years would be less severe.

In private pension funds, which now involve an enormous number of American workers, the harmful impact of compulsory retirement rules is even more devastating. The certain knowledge that monthly pension payments will start in nearly all cases at age 65 increases the gross cost of funded private pension plans substantially. It is the main reason that, in spite of the billions of dollars invested in private pension trusts covering millions of workers, average monthly payments to be recovered are so low, quite often only $60 to $70. These sums, of course, are collectible on top of Social Security.

We already have noted in the previous chapter that the largest old age insurance monthly payment that can be hoped for from Social Security by a couple retiring at age 65 is $254 and this can be obtained only if there still are dependent children. For most couples, the maximum that can be obtained is $190.50 a month. At age 62, the maximum is $174.70. Without benefits from a wife who has been employed the required number of quarters, the maximum benefit on retirement at age 65 is $127.

And these figures are only for those who can show earnings of $400 a month or more since 1950.

On top of these Social Security benefits and whatever private pension you may obtain from your employer, you are allowed to earn $1,200 a year without jeopardizing your Social Security benefits—and if you and your wife are over 65, you both get doubled personal exemptions from Federal income tax.

But even at best, chances are this is going to reduce the monthly expendable income of the retired couple to around $275 a month against a standard of living which they are used to based on take-home pay of anywhere from $600 to $1,000 a month. But the strongest argument against compulsory retirement is that it is probably the greatest single reason why so many men who have the misfortune to lose a job during their forties find it next to impossible to get another place as good as the one they have lost.

The insurance companies that write pension policies for employers, faced with the certainty of having to start pension payments to all the workers involved at age 65 because of compulsory retirement, have a strong incentive to put pressure on employers not to hire anyone over

45. So the job applicant aged 45 constantly runs into the rebuff—"Our pension plan rules won't permit us to hire you."

Lately, some large companies, big trade unions, and insurance companies have tried to meet this problem with what they call the portable pension. That means, the pension credit you have built up in one company can be transferred to the pension fund of your new employer, so he need not be concerned for pension reasons about hiring a man older than 45. But this is very difficult to accomplish. Ultimately portable pensions may become commonplace but it will take a long time to work out practical plans for them.

It is astonishing how much has been accomplished in the way of extending *private pension plans* in the past decade or so since insurance companies, trade unions, and pensions experts began pushing them in earnest. Insured pension plans for workers in tiny firms, employing as few as six workers, have been shown to be not only feasible but are being written in increasing numbers.

One insurance broker in Newark, New Jersey, wrote about $2.5 million worth of this business in six months. A typical plan worked like this: A small firm with a $50,000 a year payroll allocated 5 per cent of the payroll, or $2,500 a year, for the benefits and insurance premiums. Under recently enacted Federal law, *the net cost to the company is only $1,200 because of tax concessions* (if the company is in the 52 per cent corporate income tax bracket), and $1,750 if it is in the 30 per cent bracket.

Yet for this small outlay, the plan gives the worker a pension benefit of about 30 per cent of his monthly salary on retirement at age 65 added to his social security benefits. And during his working career, the plan also gives the employee $12,500 life insurance protection if he's a $5,000-a-year-man, or $40,000 if he's the $15,000 boss.

All these little firm insured pension plans include the boss. That's another point in their favor. They give workers and the boss an additional community of interest and additional incentive to work together to make the firm go.

Nevertheless, it is clear from what I have shown you in this book that for the young couple, *planning for a pension is not so profitable in the long run as simply planning from the beginning to make a success of your working career, of saving money to get a stake and investing it wisely.*

Any pension, annuity or Social Security plan has to be paid for out of your earnings. It cannot bring as much returns as do savings wisely invested in growth investments over a long period of years.

Next to the question of how to get a retirement income is the question of *where to retire* in order to live in the drastically reduced circumstances retirement entails for all except the quite successful.

The magazines and newspapers are filled with advertisements of places offering cheap *retirement sites.* The claims are totally misleading more often than not. If they are not misleading, they fail to take into account the probability that you are not the type of person who could endure the kind of existence the ad is talking about.

So the only real answer to the problem is—*Don't retire at all if you are not forced to and do not have the savings to retire comfortably.*

The best advice I can give anyone about facing the hazards of retirement is to prepare for it by having some new interest in life, preferably one that produces an income. But if you don't want an extra income in retirement at least have an interest that will take up your time and keep you happy.

Write a book, start a mail order business, learn something you can teach to others—become an investment counselor, or a salesman for some useful product or service.

Or, if you can afford it, become a real enthusiast at some hobby that is intellectually demanding and stimulating.

So, bear in mind . . .

It's up to each individual to plan his later years. Some unpleasantness, as forced retirement, can not be helped. But retirement can be the beginning of a new adventure; it can also be a grim thing if you have not given thought to what you will do, beforehand.

Private pension plans, which can supplement Social Security payments or can provide funds where there is no Social Security, are not expensive to the companies that have them as the tax benefits are heavy.

All things considered, don't retire if you can avoid it and if you don't wish to retire.

If you do retire—keep living. Use your imagination to find a satisfying, even a profitable, occupation.

25. Inevitable Inflation

"The poor we have with us always."

Also inflation.

Many people who howl about inflation do not realize that it is inevitable. The truth is that the trend of economy in the Western world has been inflationary for a thousand years—perhaps longer.

Politicians, economists or business men who think otherwise are acting much as King Canute did when he commanded the waves to subside at his royal wish.

Why is this so?

It is so because the material conditions of life and society improve steadily over the centuries and the improvement has to be paid for. We pay for them by slow inflation; it is the only way mankind can pay for them. For inflation is a reflex of increased productivity.

Our planet does not contain anything on which we can put a constant value. Gold is the nearest thing we have and its relative constant value is maintained only with great difficulty and for comparatively short periods of time. There never has been enough gold on Earth to maintain a constant value for money over long periods.

The amount of money one pound of gold will put in circulation has grown enormously over the centuries. Here, in the United States, we have had to double the number of dollars in a pound of gold in our own time. Other countries have had to go to much greater lengths.

So, people who talk about inflation as if it could be halted permanently, simply don't know what they are saying.

Of course the inflationary course of history has not been uninterrupted. There have been periods of stability lasting a century and short periods of extremely drastic deflation like our Great Depression of 1929-33. Historians and economists usually write about the disastrous effects of inflation on a single era or a single country. When inflation assumes runaway proportions, as it has in so much of the world as a result of the two World Wars in our century, the consequences are dire indeed to those who have to live through it.

But curiously, society seems able to make great economic, scientific and social strides forward right in the midst of even severe inflationary conditions.

On the other hand, what records we have of those times in past centuries when money was remarkably stable for protracted periods and wages and prices were firmly fixed by royal decree show clearly that, during these eras, man made virtually no forward progress in any field— neither economic, scientific, social nor political. Society simply stagnated in stability. If there is anything that proves the capitalist contention that risk is a fundamental of human dynamism, it is this fact.

Reflecting on this, we are virtually forced to conclude that *slow but steady inflation is the basic method by which human society finances the cost of its own advancement.*

Recently several books have appeared which seek to explain the remarkable prosperity of the age that produced the great cathedrals of Europe and the poverty of the immediately succeeding centuries in terms of failure of the rulers and peoples of those time to understand the inevitable shortage of gold and consequent need for slow inflation.

One of these books is by Dr. Hugo R. Fack.* Another

* *The Gothic,* by Dr. Hugo R. Fack, Free Economy Press, San Antonio, Texas.

is by Arthur Dahlberg of Columbia University, who is president of the Econometric Institute.* These books show clearly that, in the 12th and 13th centuries, Europe was remarkably prosperous. They argue that the prosperity was brought about by the practice of "seignorage," a systematic reissuing of gold and silver coin with a heavy tax, 10 per cent or more, levied for new minting. The effect of this tax was to make hoarding impractical, and to force all the currency into regular use. Hoarded coin would lose value just as hoarded paper money loses value nowadays in times of inflation; seignorage, in effect, was a way of slowly and systematically inflating the prices of gold and silver. And according to these writers, it worked amazingly well.

Why was it abandoned? According to the historians, the process was totally misunderstood by the people and there was constant clamor for its abolition and the introduction of permanent money. The barons and very rich feared that the masses were becoming too prosperous and that what they regarded as the natural order of society would be subverted.

So the barons and the rich had their way. "Seignorage" was abolished, the values of money and the prices of goods were generally frozen, trade languished, monopolies flourished and Europe began a period of centuries of relative poverty while rulers and bankers sat on the lid trying to prevent that natural slow inflationary trend of history.

But inflation does not move on a wide or uniform front. That is what confuses people. In spite of the overall inflationary course of history, an astonishingly large part of the economy moves in the opposite direction at the same time because of technology. Manufactured goods of all kinds become cheaper and more plentiful right in the midst of creeping inflation. So does food, which, more

* *Money in Motion,* by Arthur Dahlberg, John De Graff, New York, 1962.

and more, moves out of the realm of feudal agrarian economics to become governed by the economics of manufacturing.

But the gross costs of government, education, health care, defense, public safety and most other goods and services goes up constantly. On the other hand, *the cost of energy* in the form of electricity goes down, and so does the net cost of transportation.

However, the two vital elements in the economic base of any society—land and manpower—get ever more expensive. *Land has to become more expensive as the population increases.* Manpower, whether executive, professional, or labor, has to grow more expensive as the standard of living rises. More than anything else, it is the rising prices of land and manpower that make inflation a reflex, even a function, of human progress.

Economists and corporation executives and even politicians are fond of talking about the need to tie wage increases to increased productivity. Within the reference frame of the particular industrial problems these people are talking about, they usually are justified in taking such a stand.

But, in the long run, wages cannot be tied to productivity increase in a given company or industry. The shoe is on the other foot, something far too many management people do not realize. The working man has struggled upwards over the centuries from a slavery in which his employer held power of life and death over him and considered it unprofitable to keep him after about his thirty-fifth year.

Even after two thousand years, these memories linger in the class subconsciousness of the working man and to this very day, even in the United States, this feeling affects the attitude of labor towards employers. The working man still is determined to take away from the propertied class a share of what it holds. Labor will not settle for an improvement in its standard of living equivalent only to the improvement in the employer's business. What it really boils down to is that, in order to survive, a given company or industry must increase its productivity and profitability sufficiently to meet the irresistible demands of labor. For it is labor that ultimately holds the power—not management.

Of course, since you cannot grab something that does not exist, the whole working force of the nation has to settle for an improvement in the standard of living, equivalent to the growth of the national economy. In that sense, wages can be tied to increased productivity. But, *the employer who thinks it is up to his laborers to increase productivity is suffering from a fatal delusion.*

As to labor holding the decisive power, let us reflect. The argument often heard that scientists, engineers, scholars and great philosophers and statesmen have played the truly decisive roles in the long drama of history is persuasive. But the sober weight of evidence is in favor of the view that it was the upward struggle of the masses that applied the decisive power. The slave of two thousand years ago who slew his master with a club and fled to freedom in the forest and the union leader of today who forces big wage concessions from a huge industry— they have been the real star players on the stage of history.

Moreover, the aristocracy of birth and military glory of past times did not produce many of the creative minds that changed the world so over the centuries. Even in the ancient world, many of the best philosophers, artists, scientists and engineers came from the ranks of the commoner.

I have gone into the *inevitability of continued inflation* at some length to make it clear that everyone who hopes to get along in the world must learn to spend his income with long range inflationary trends in mind.

These trends particularly affect spending to produce

income and to create an estate to leave to our children. Life insurance policies, mortgages and bonds, both foreign and domestic, are valued in fixed amounts of money. We need to know how to estimate how much long range inflationary trends affect their ultimate values as savings or protection.

Common stocks, land, houses and going businesses are not valued in fixed amounts of money. So long as they are healthy values in themselves they automatically gain in money value with inflation.

So do many things we do not buy primarily as investments but only for use and pleasure—jewelry, paintings and works of art and fine furniture for example. Even an automobile can be worth more when it is thirty years old than it cost new *if* it happens to be a rare example of fine engineering and carriage design, as the famous Duesenbergs of the early 1930s.

The catch is to find out which of these things that can adjust themselves automatically to inflation over the years are the healthy values that will do so. In fact, with the exception of land and good common stocks, the odds are against any given purchase going up much in value.

Even in land and common stocks, it is frighteningly easy to pick a loser. Land values in most parts of the United States have gone up tremendously throughout our national history. But in many rural sections and in some parts of every city the appreciation is so slow and so herky-jerky in relation to the cost of paying taxes and otherwise carrying the property that the land has to be considered a poor investment. It's easy to buy almost worthless land only a few blocks away from extremely valuable lots.

Similarly, the over-all trend of common stocks, whether they are dividend income shares like those of the huge American Telephone & Telegraph Company or sensational growth shares such as those of many of the better capital stock life insurance companies, has been upward in most of our history. But as bank trust officers warn people constantly—"It takes great time and patience and care to invest profitably in common stocks."

Moreover, all the so-called growth investments, stocks, real estate and personal property, are subject to the violent dips caused by recessions and technological change. Hence, there is a huge element of risk in them during any given generation. The risk is so great that often investments in life insurance policies, bonds and mortgages in fixed dollar valuations produce more beneficial gain to the family.

But it's well to remember that mortgages and bonds can be defaulted. In times past, defaults in these fixed value securities have been about as big a source of loss as worthless stocks. Even in the first quarter of this century the losses from defaulted bonds of all kinds were tremendous—particularly from foreign government bonds.

The general solution to the problem of inevitable inflation is obvious—but not so easy to carry out. *No one should put all his eggs in either the growth basket or in the bond basket.* In spending money to produce income and leave an estate for wife and children, you must learn how to choose and buy both things that have safe fixed values and things that likely will grow and grow in value over the years.

I have tried to make it clear that whenever you make any major expenditure of money, whether to produce income or just to make life more comfortable and pleasant for yourself or your family, deciding how to do it right is not easy. It involves looking before you leap—or, rather, before you spend.

In truth, it is always hard to spend money.